MEXICAN FOLK ART

COLORING BOOK

MARTY NOBLE

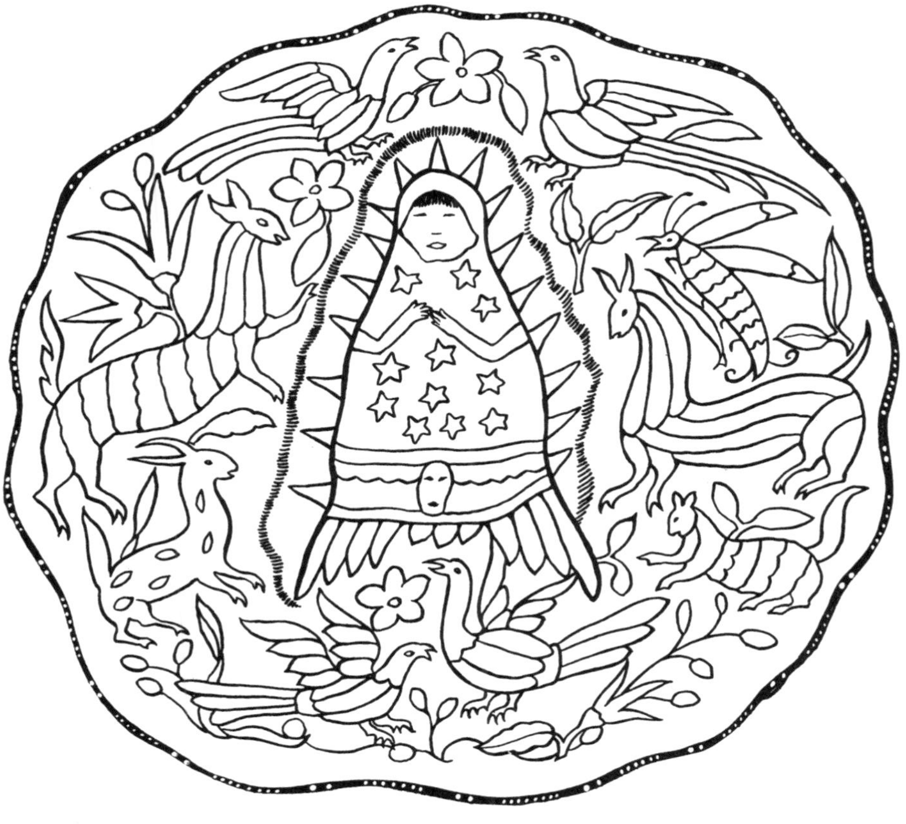

DOVER PUBLICATIONS, INC.
MINEOLA, NEW YORK

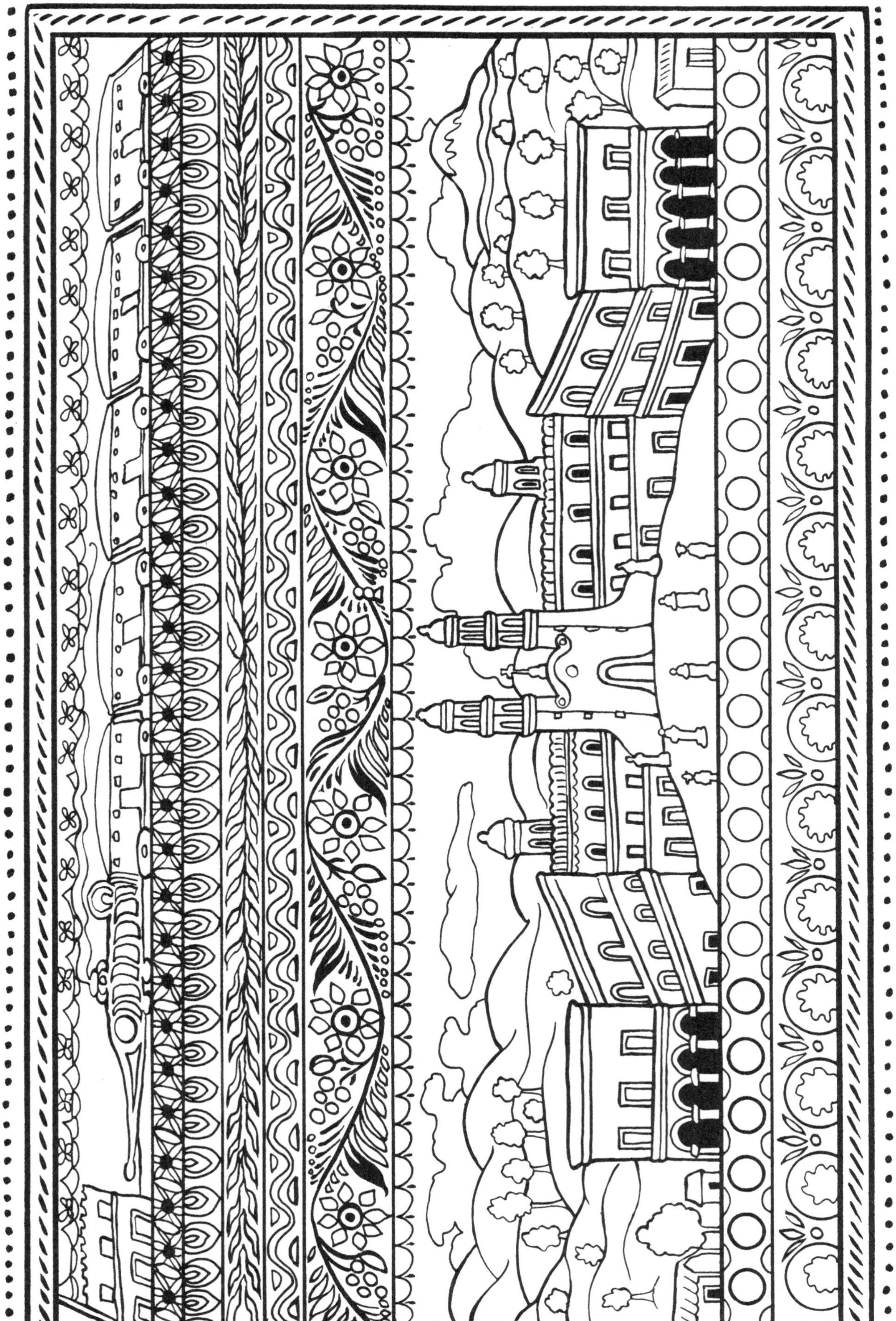

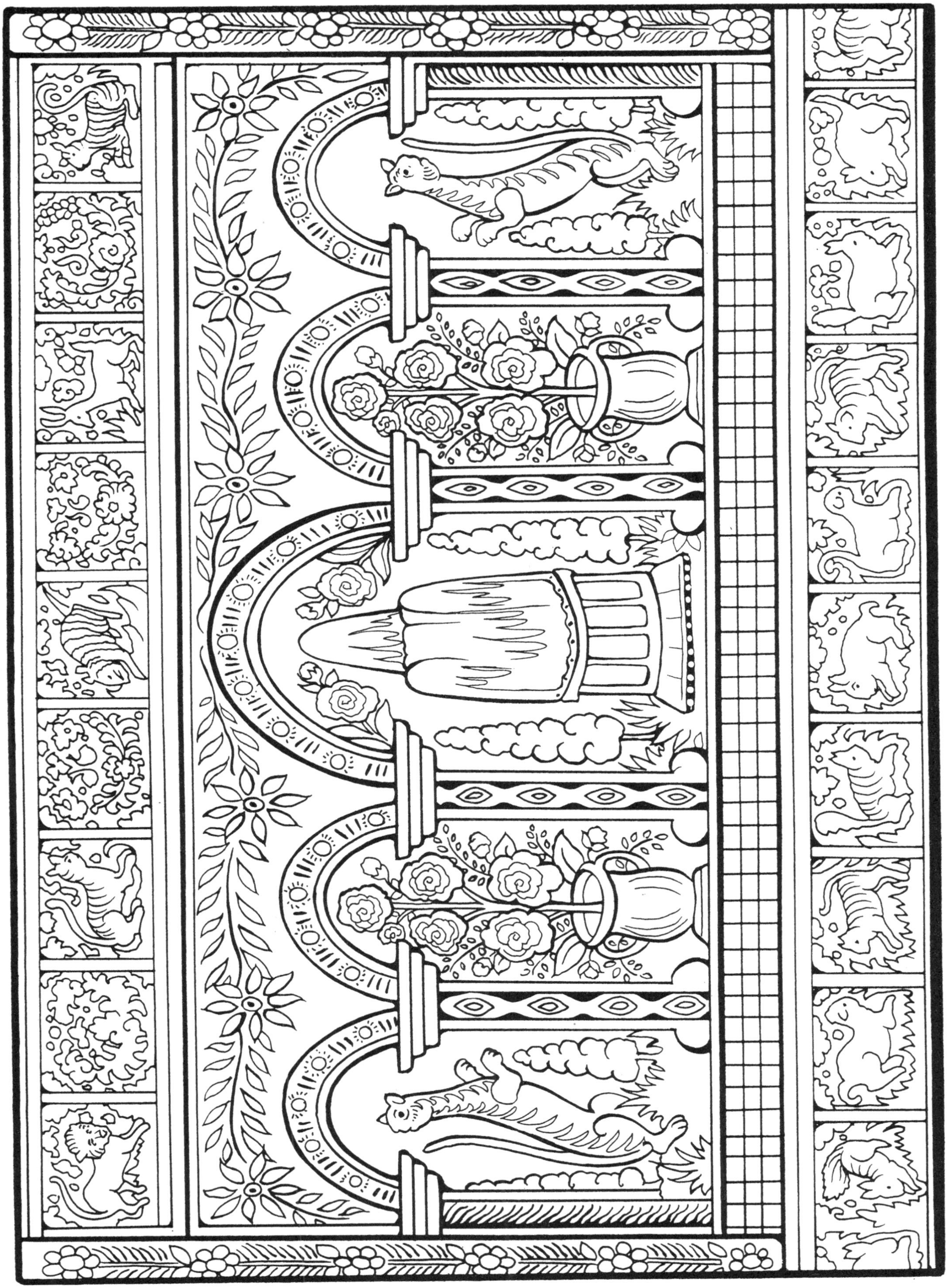

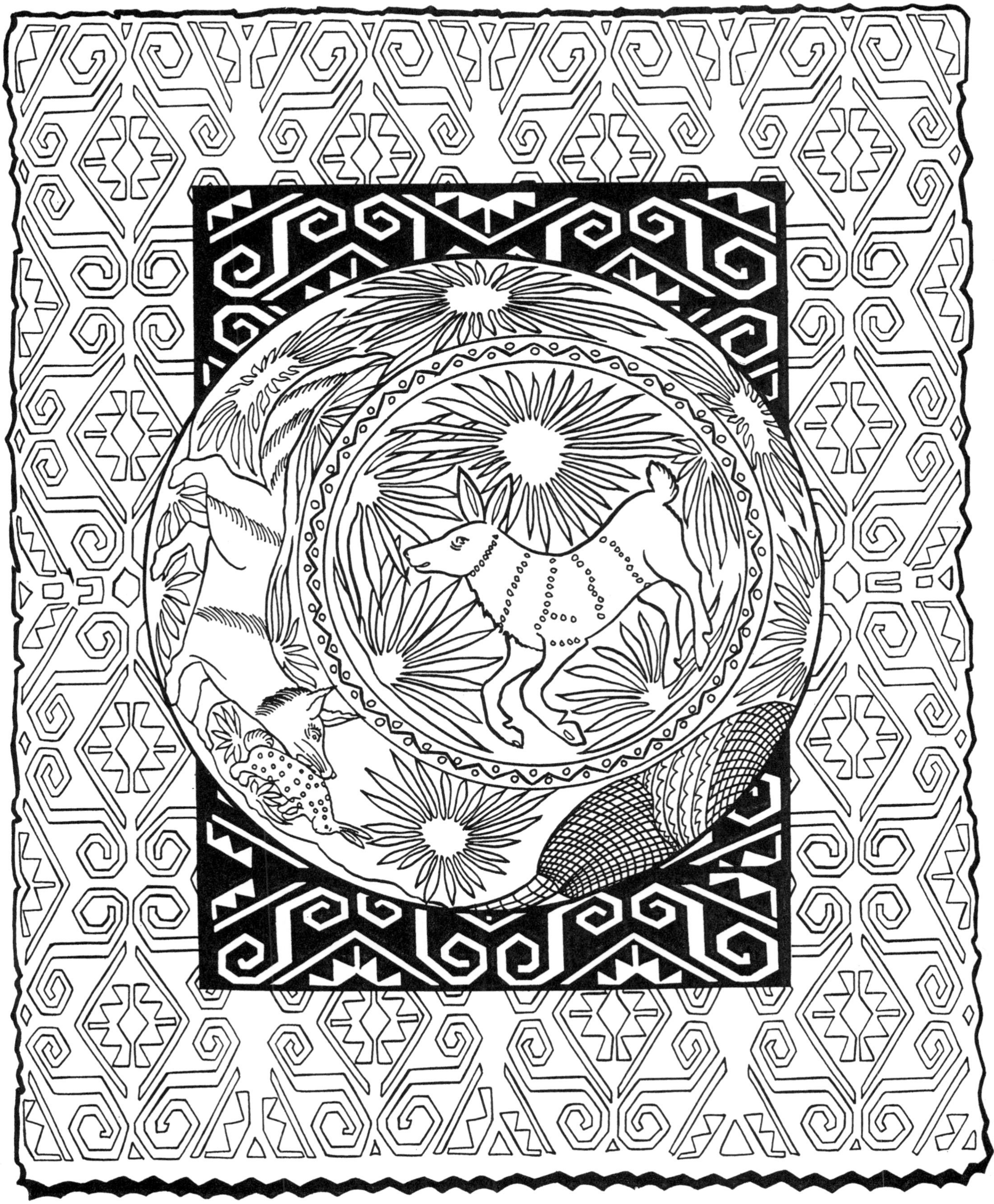

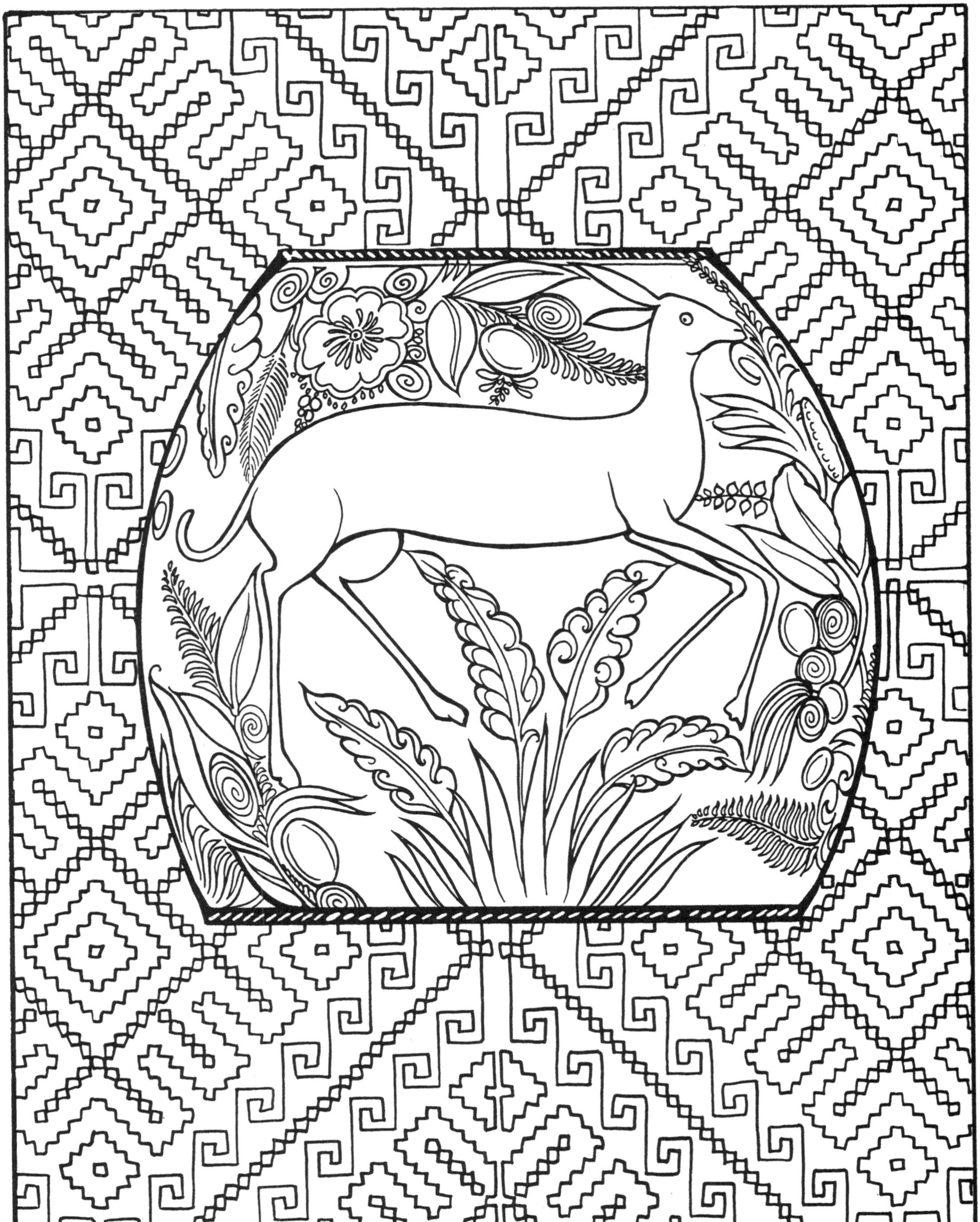

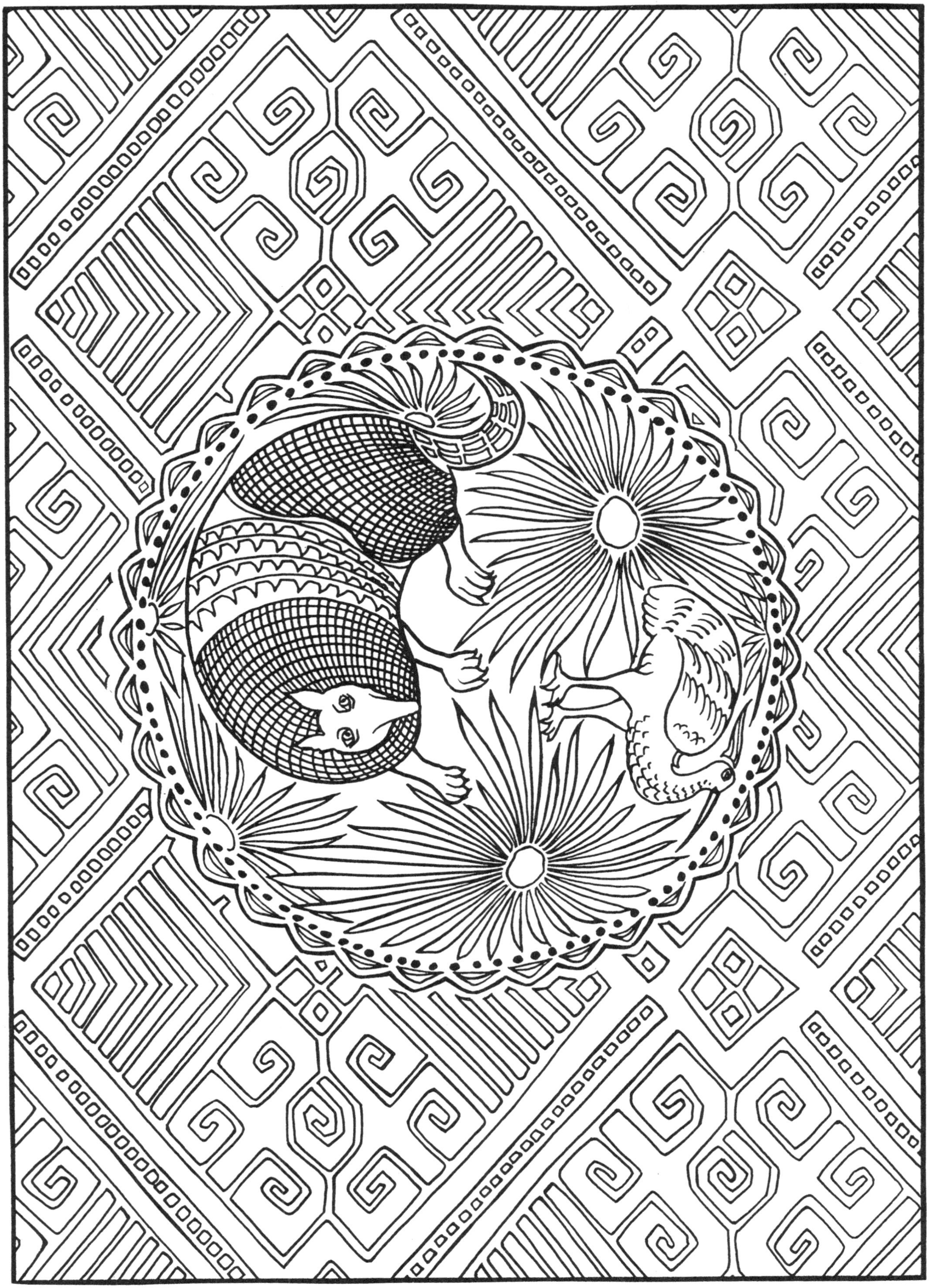

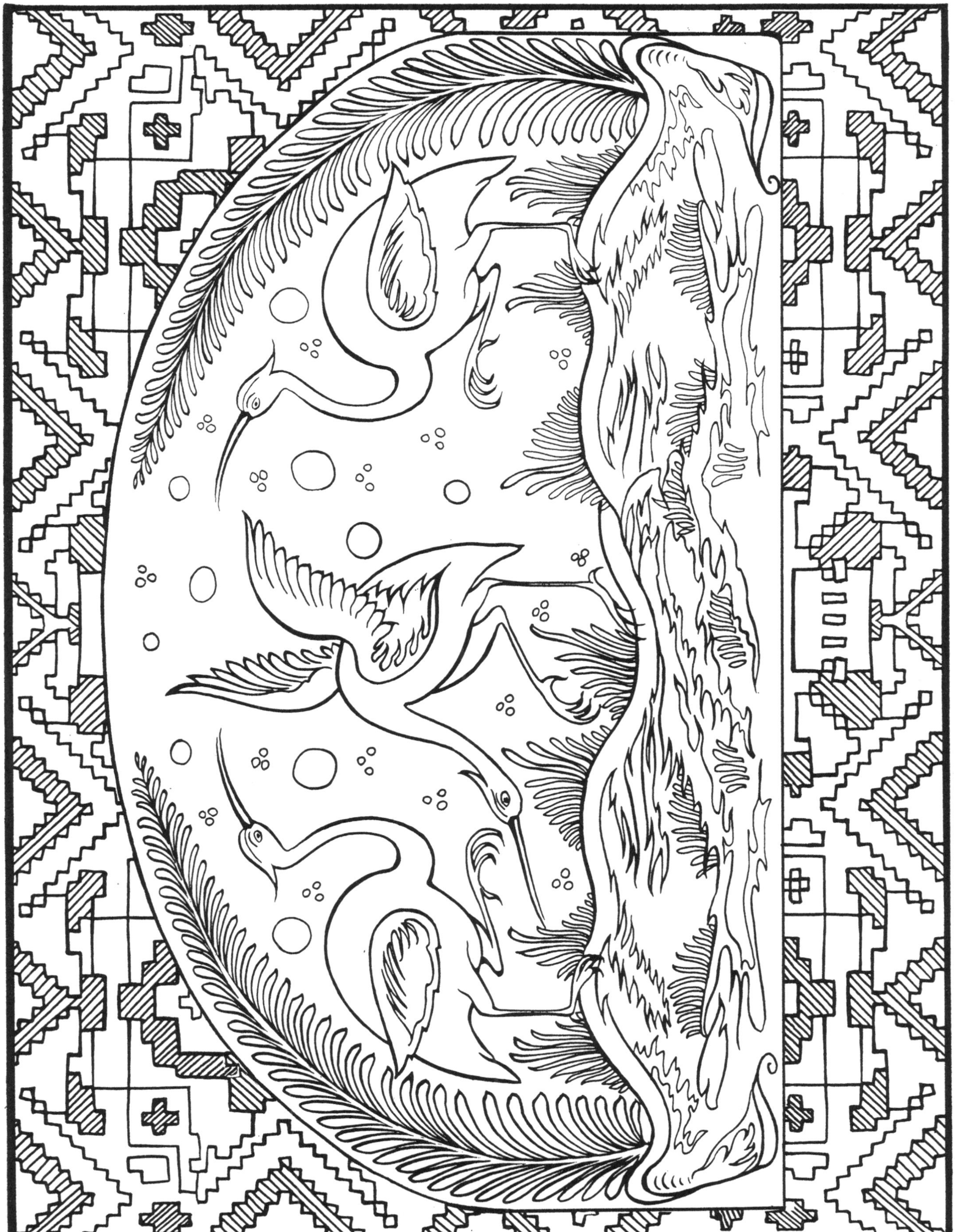

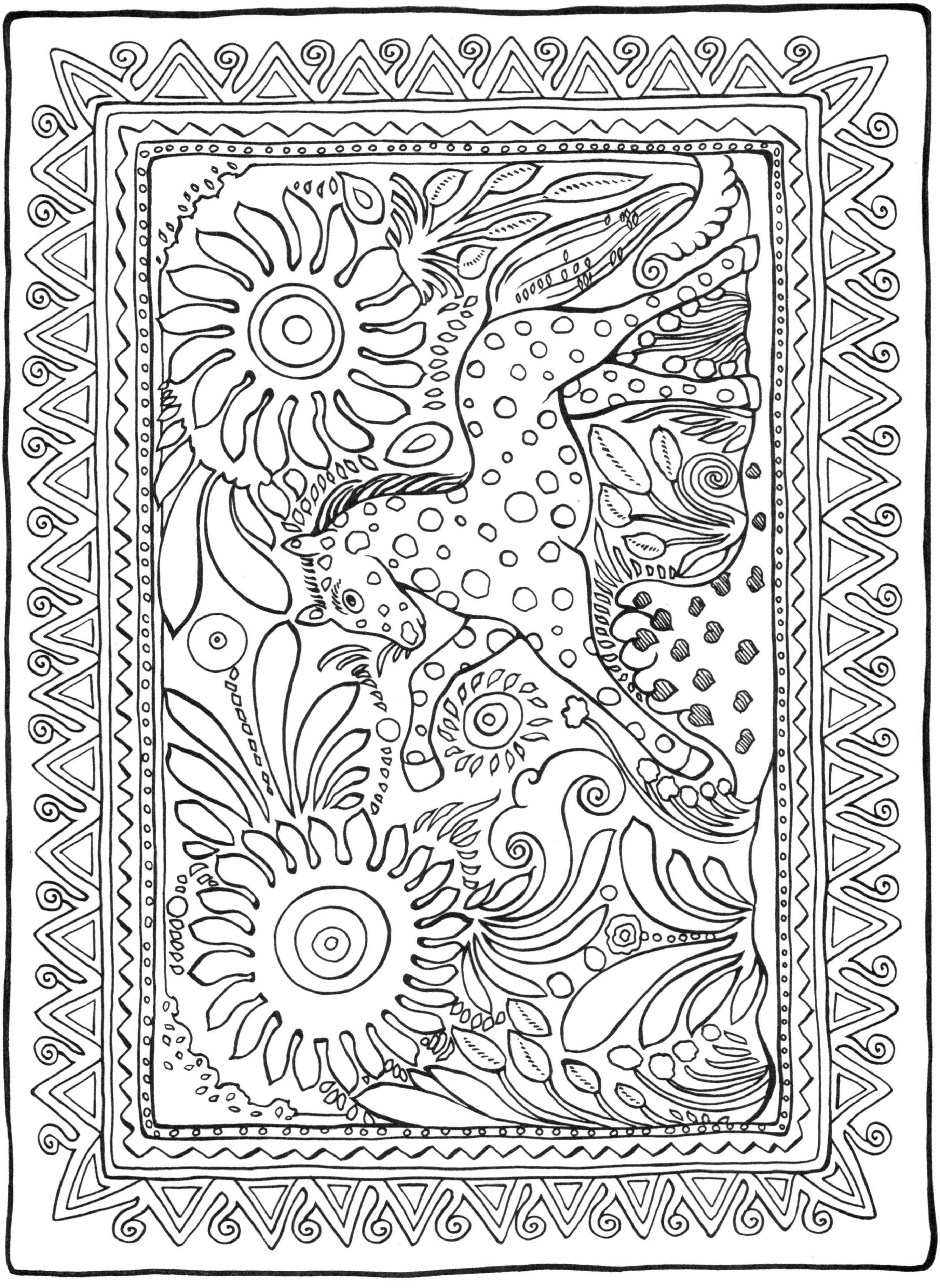

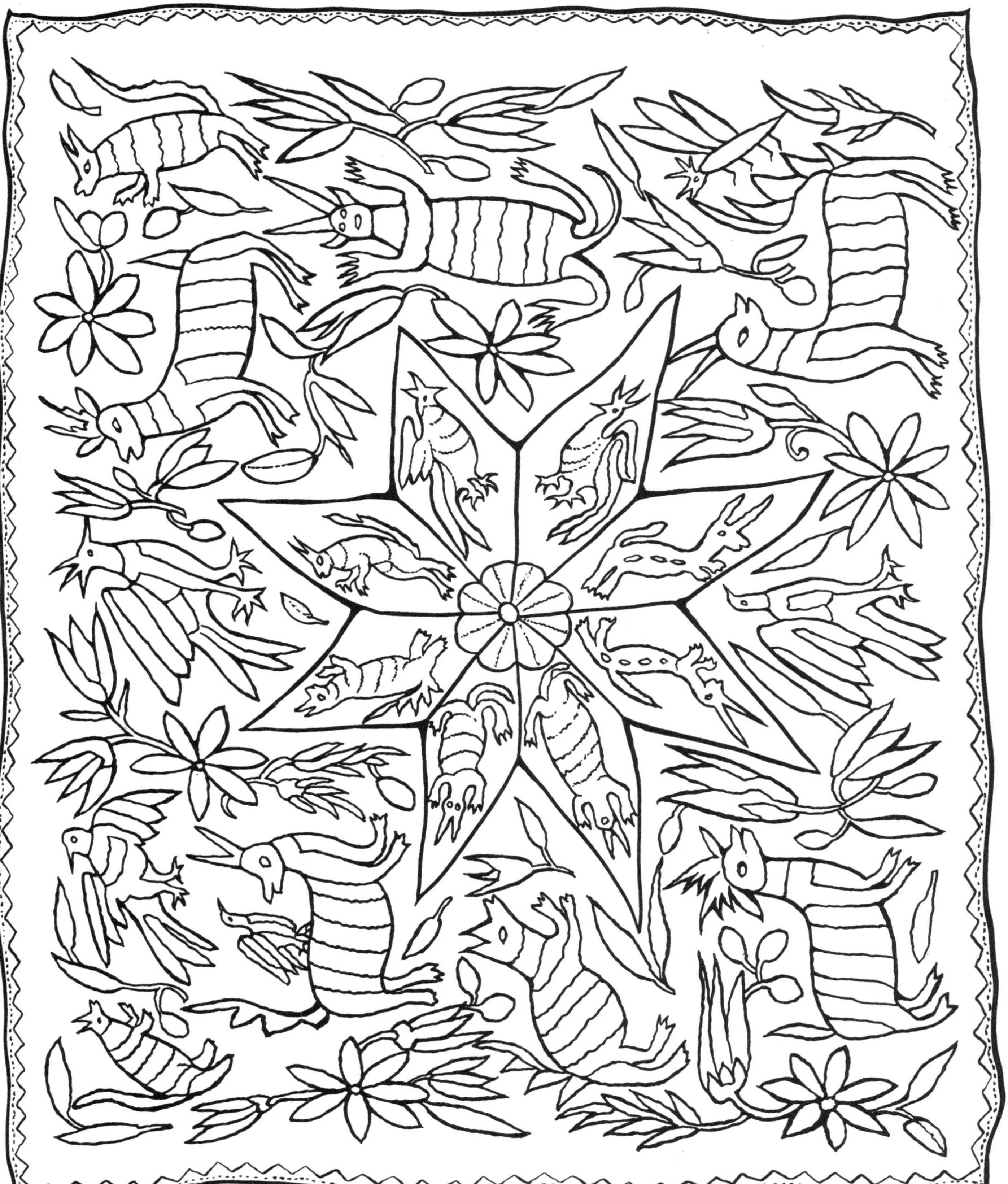

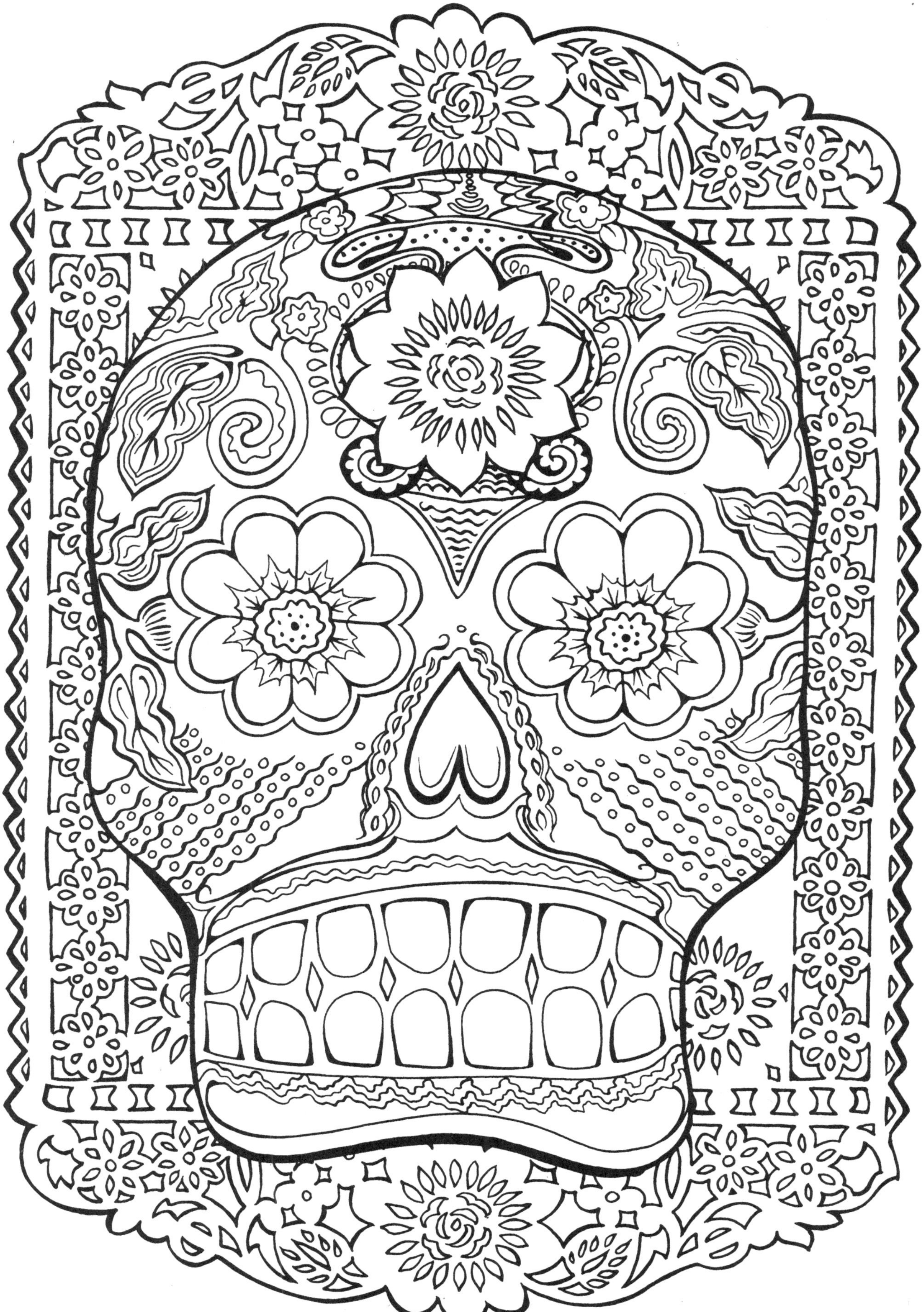

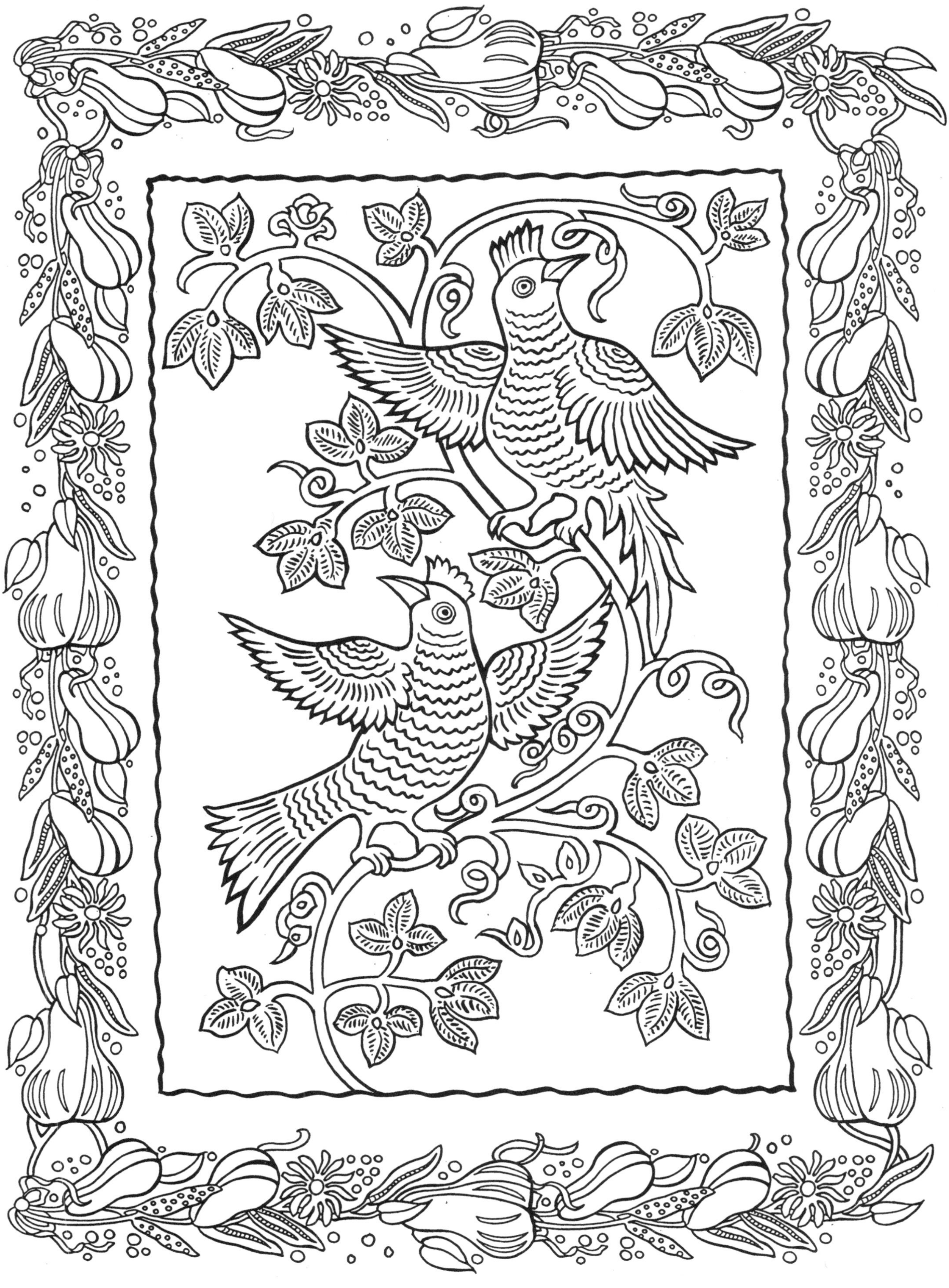

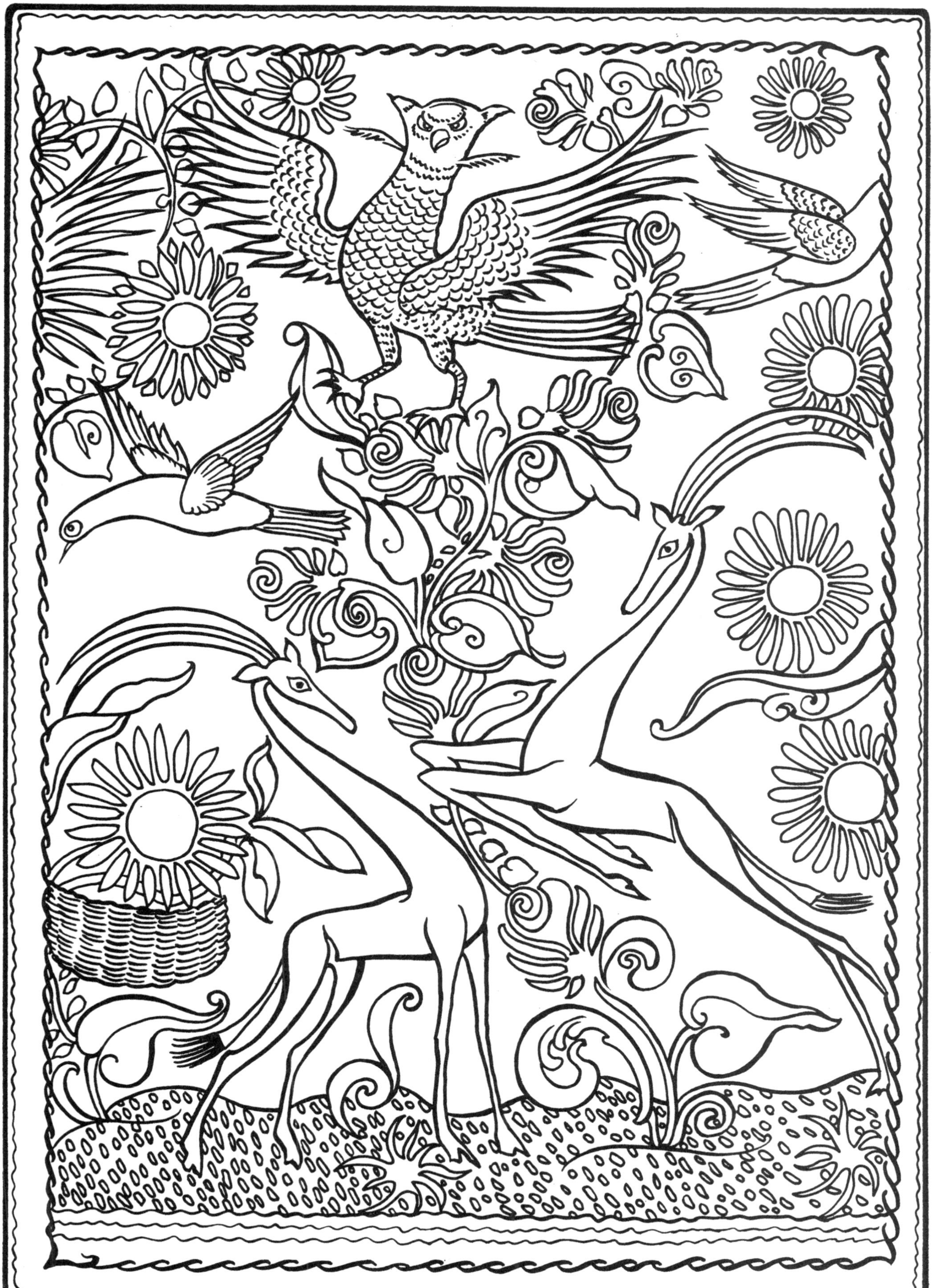

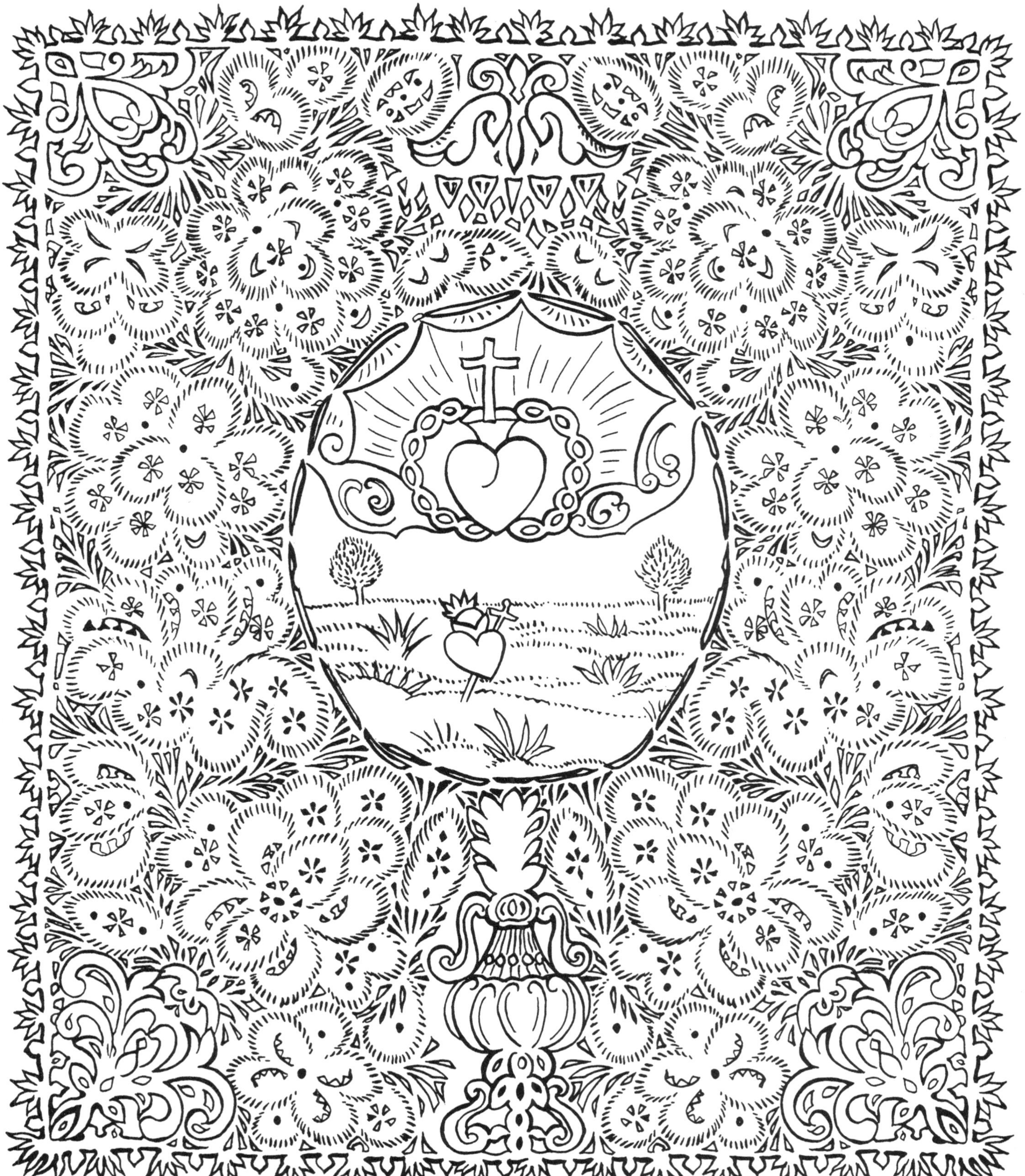

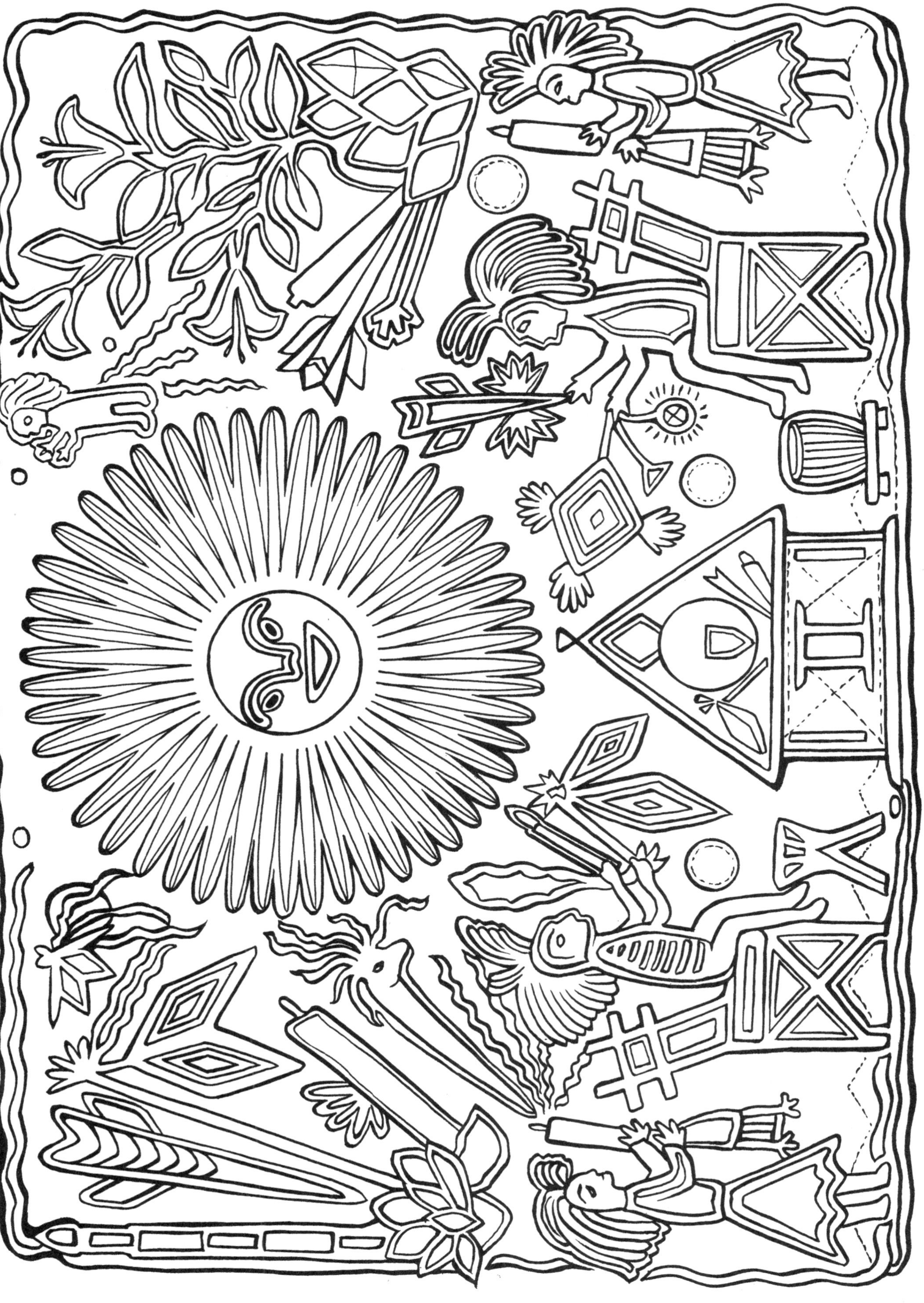

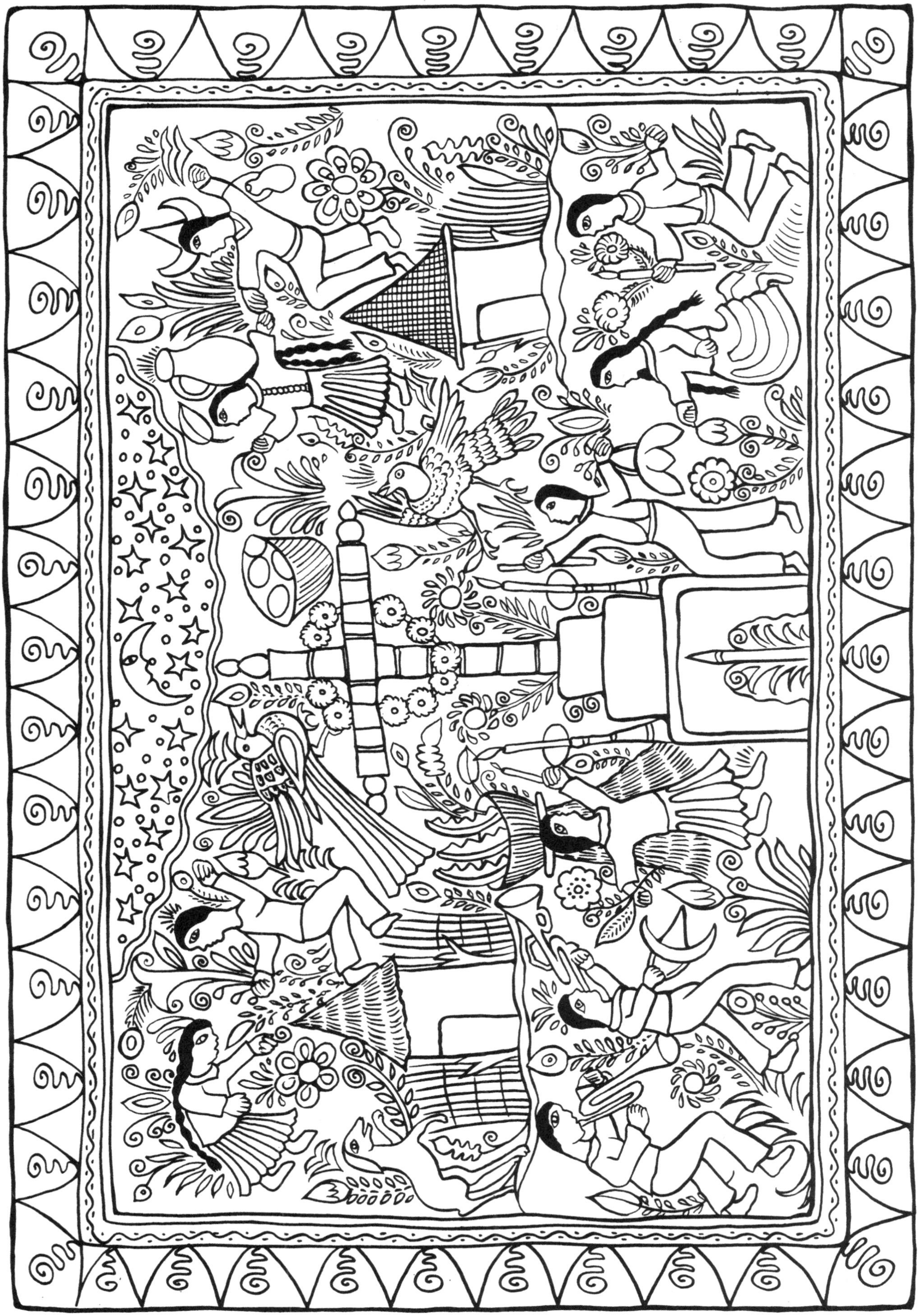

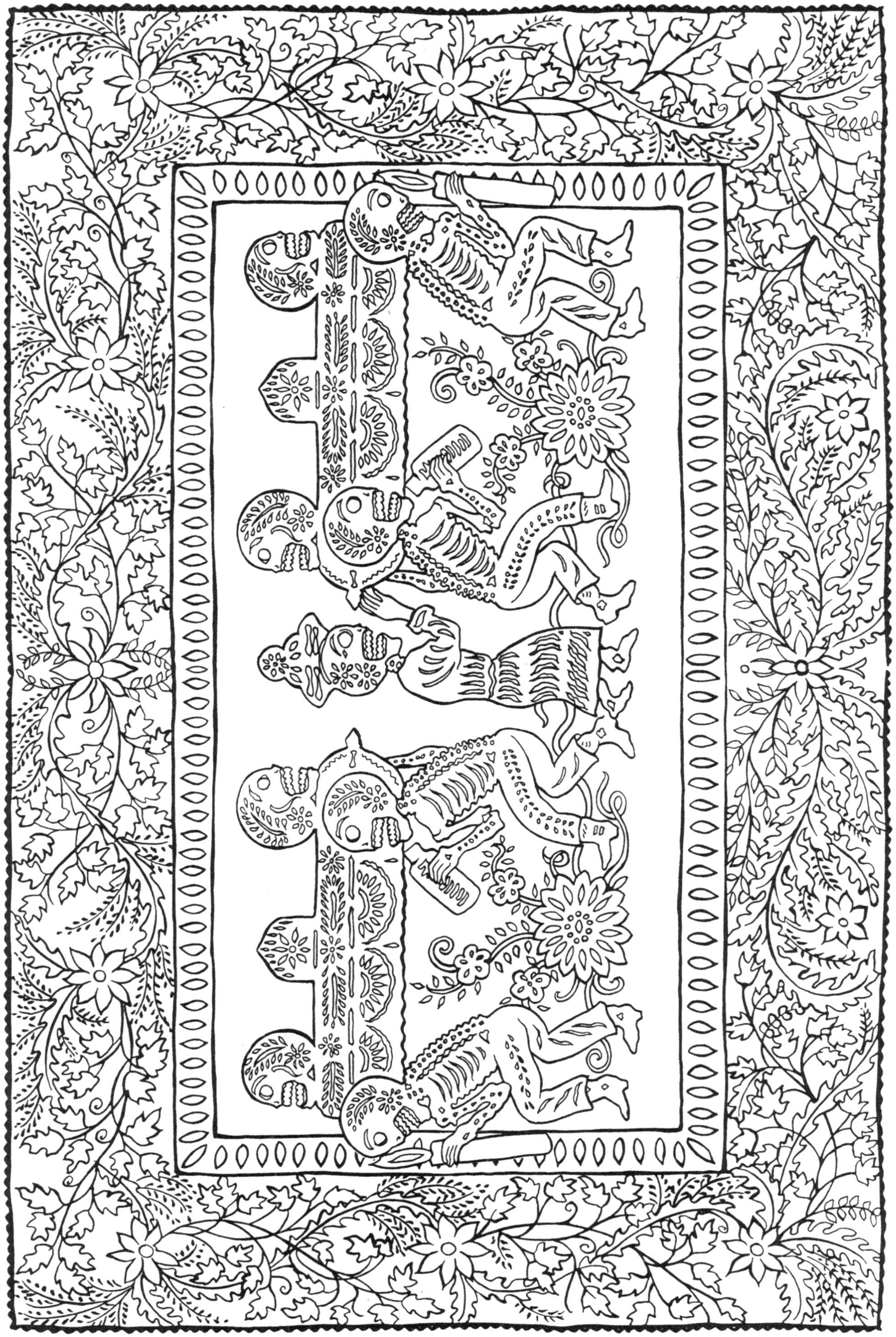

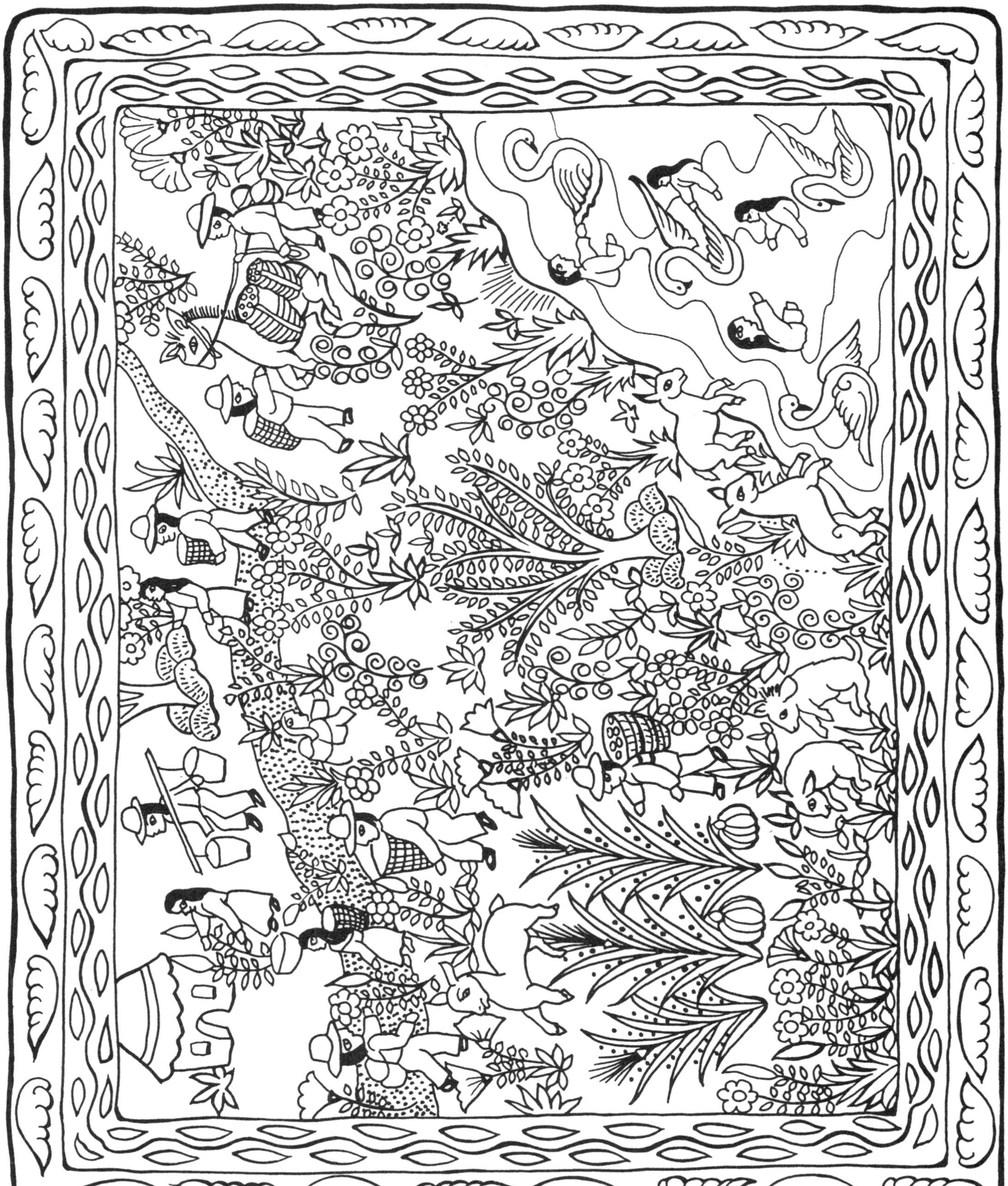

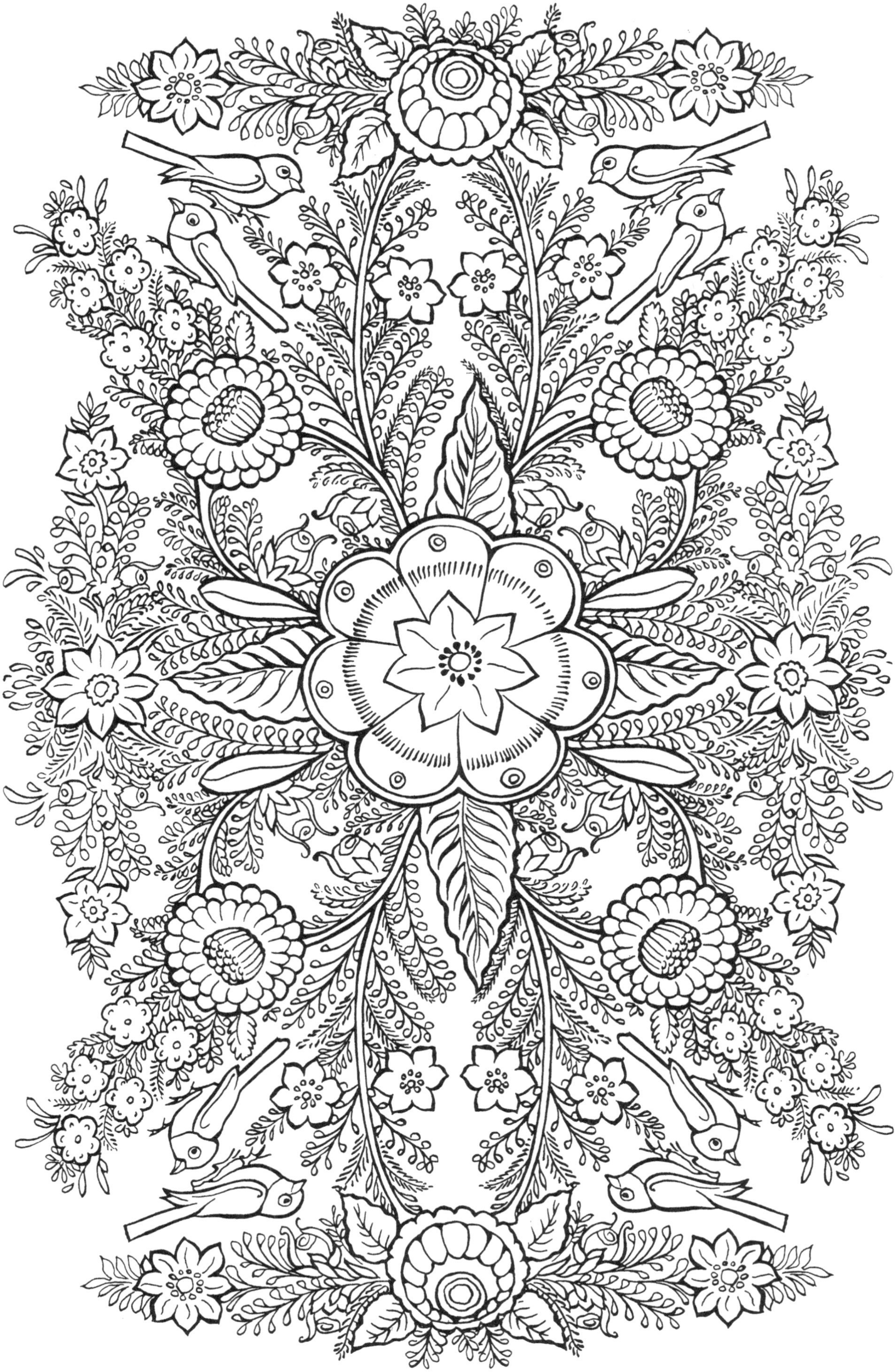

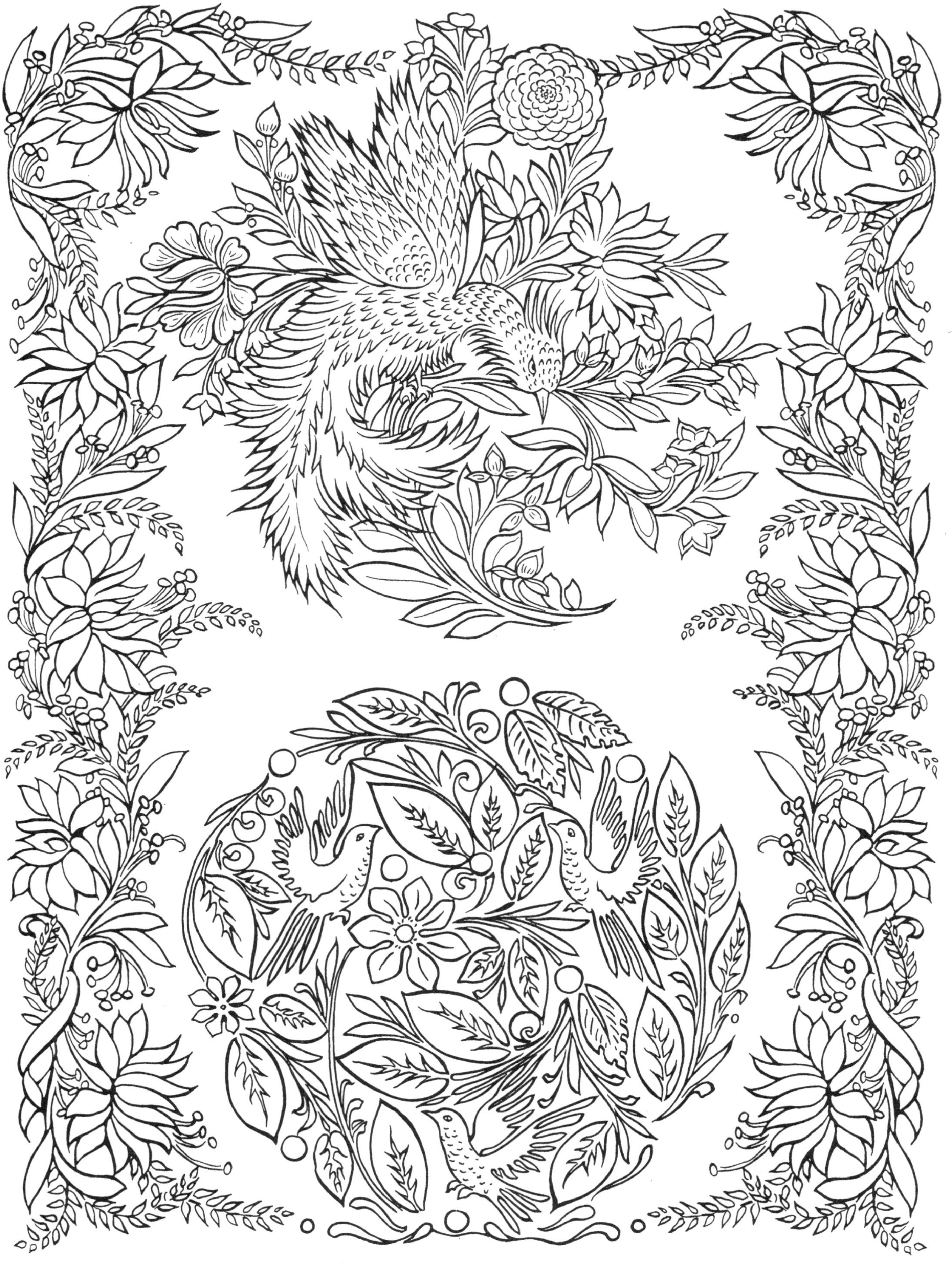

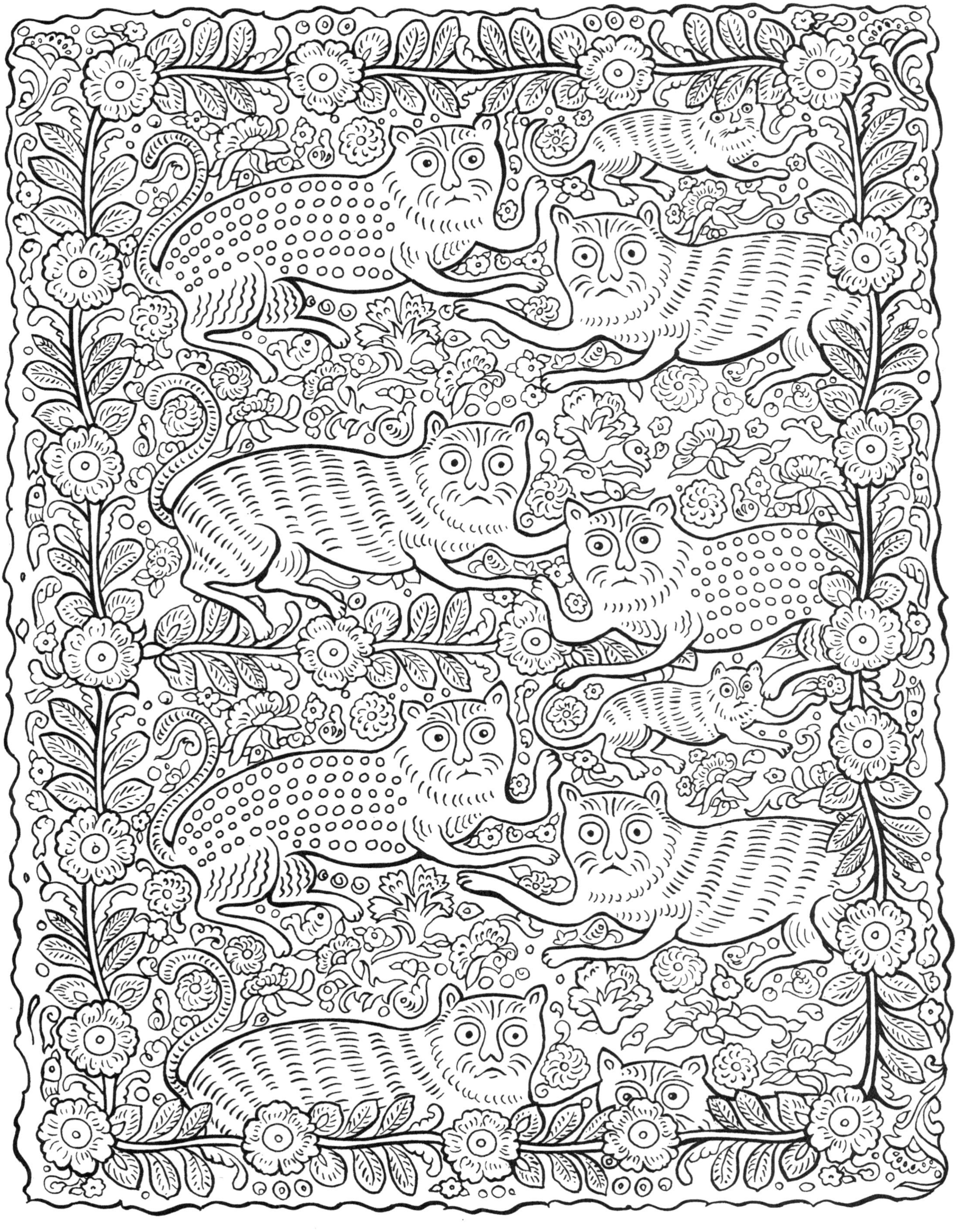

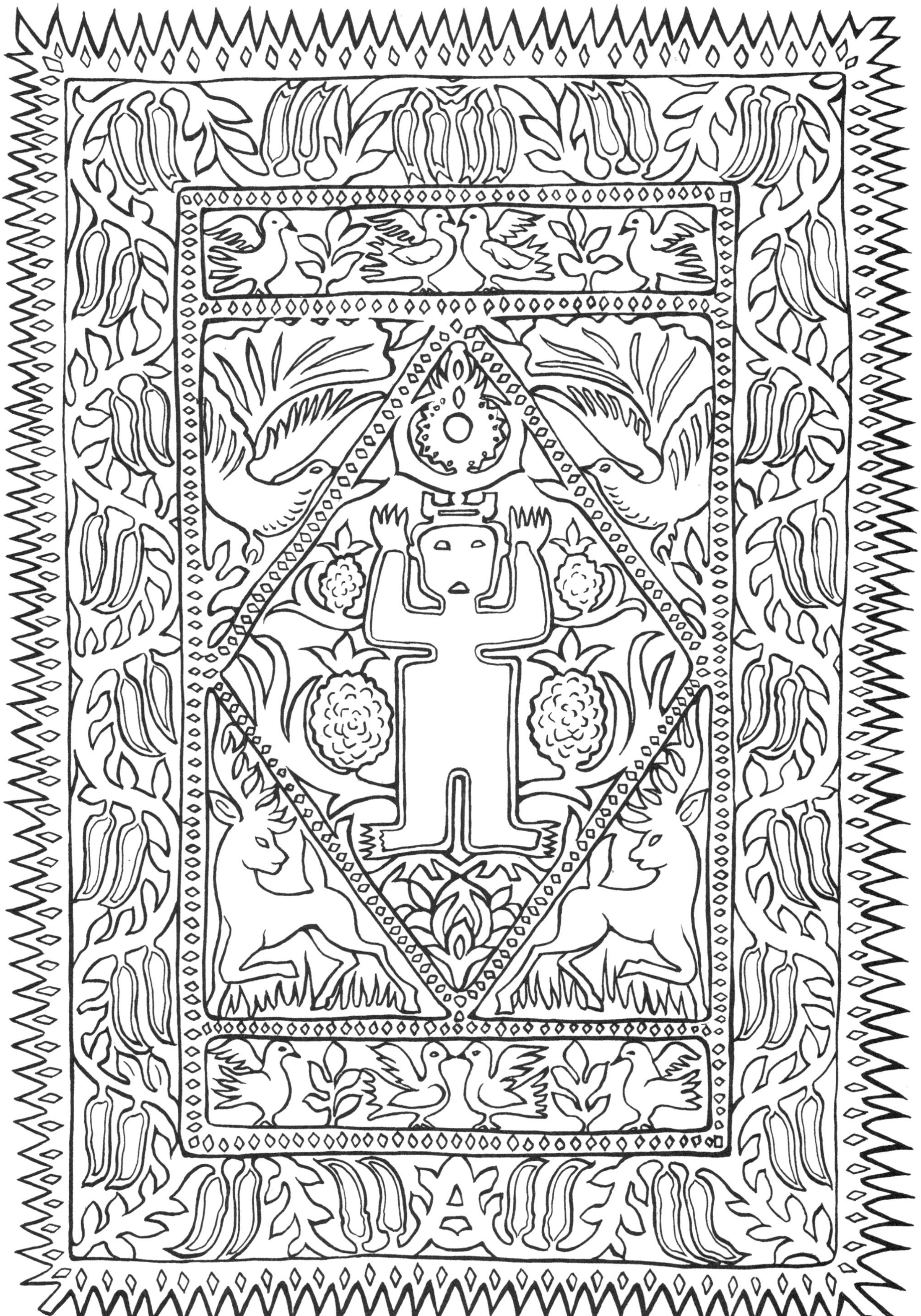

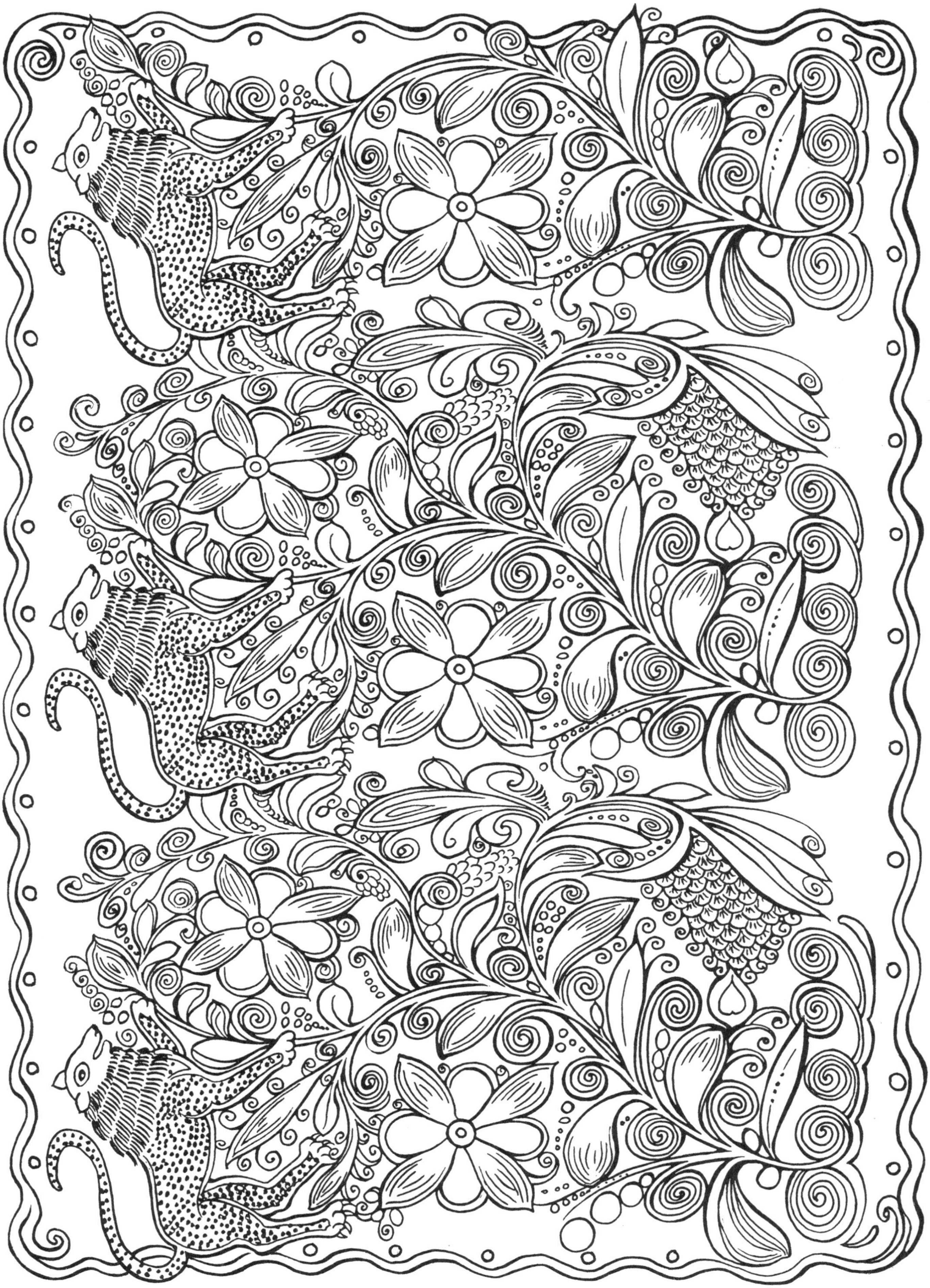

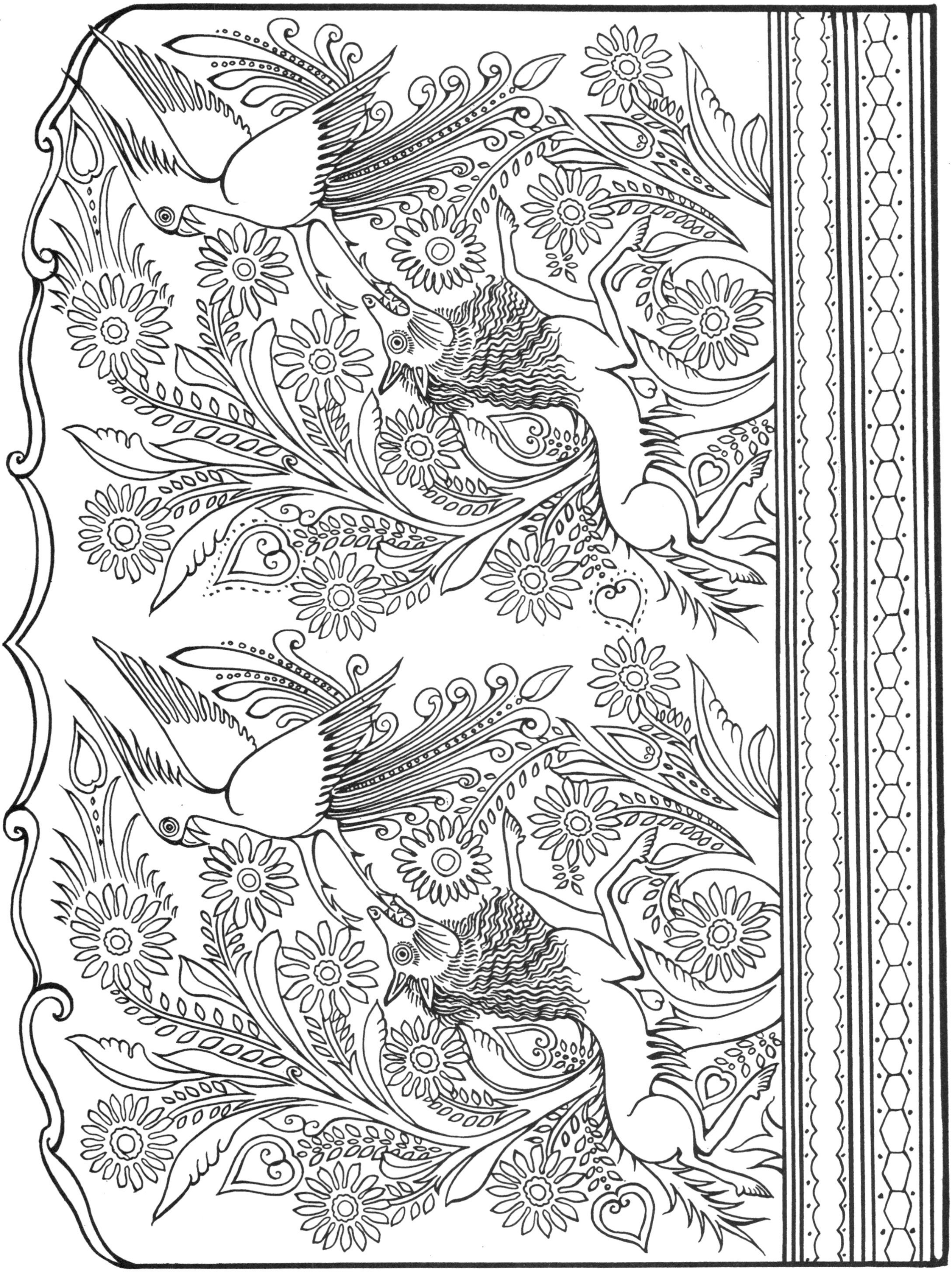

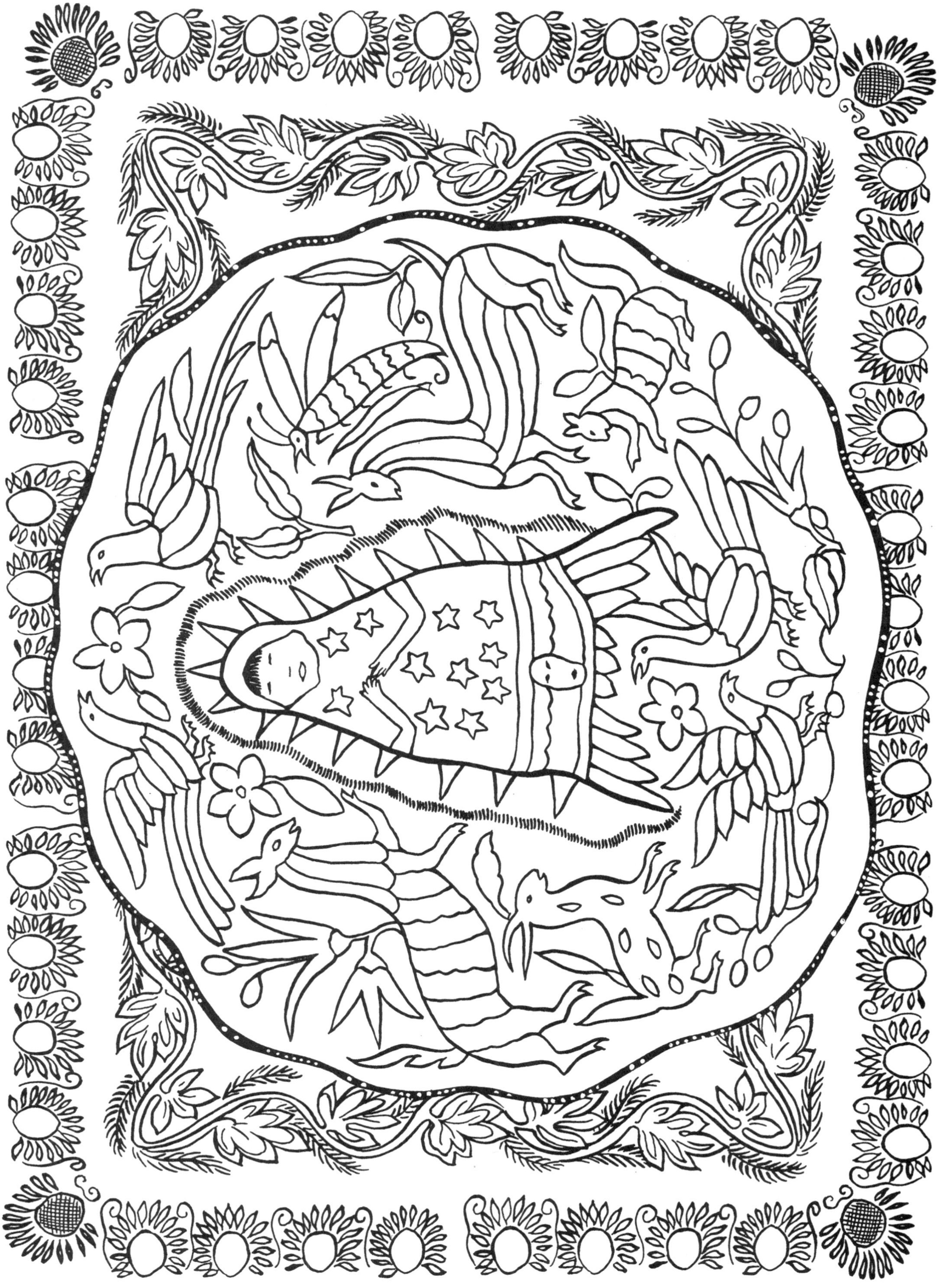

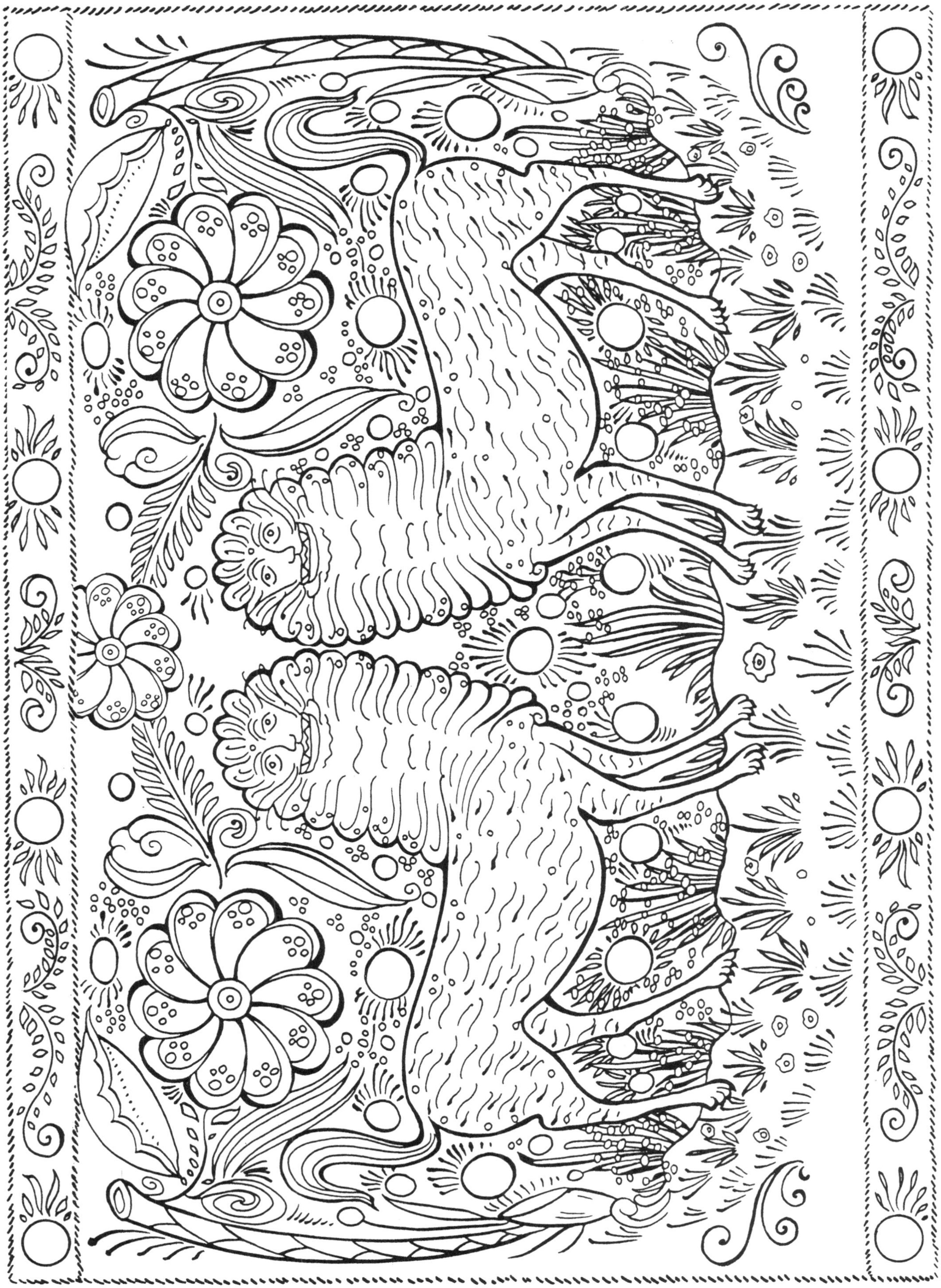

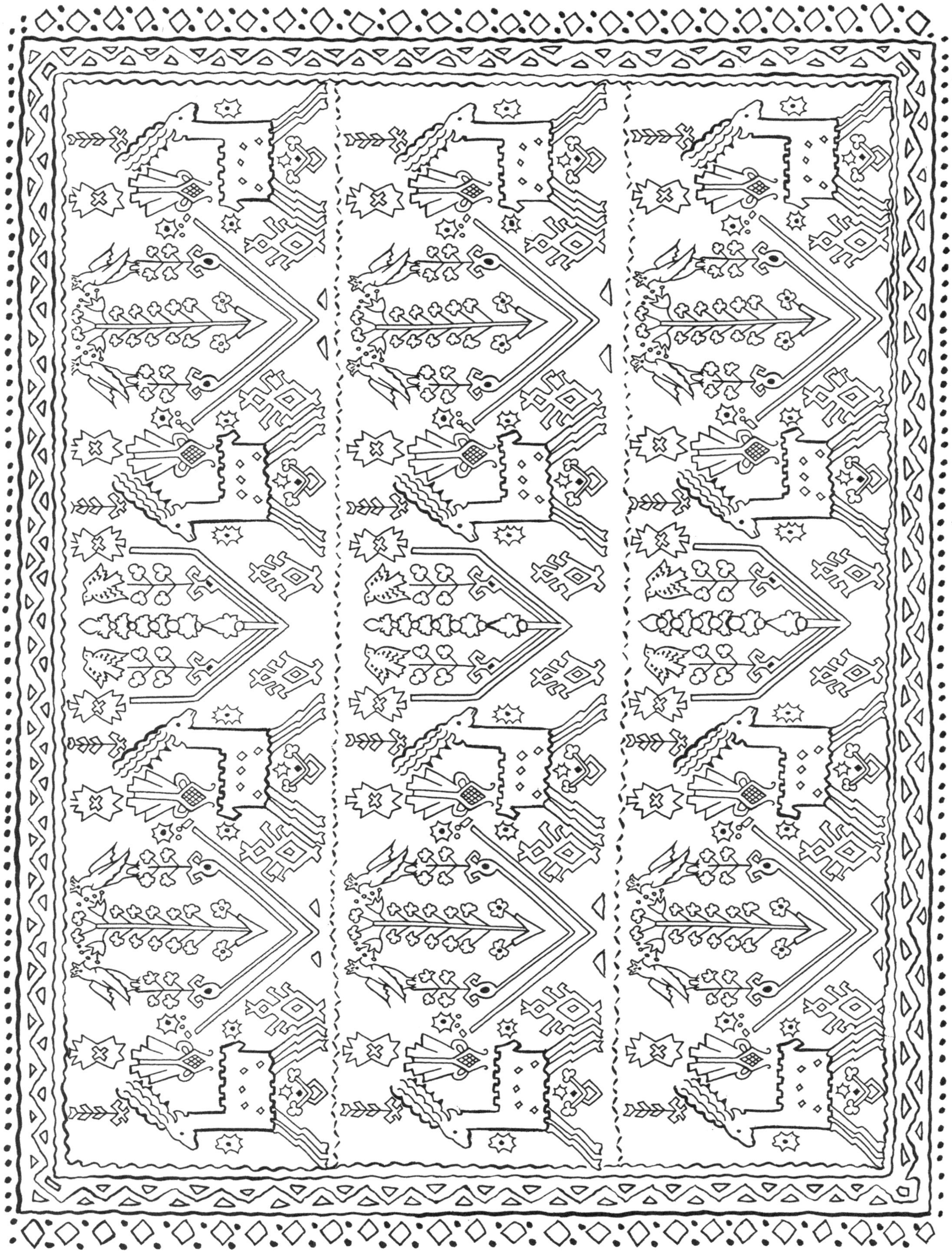

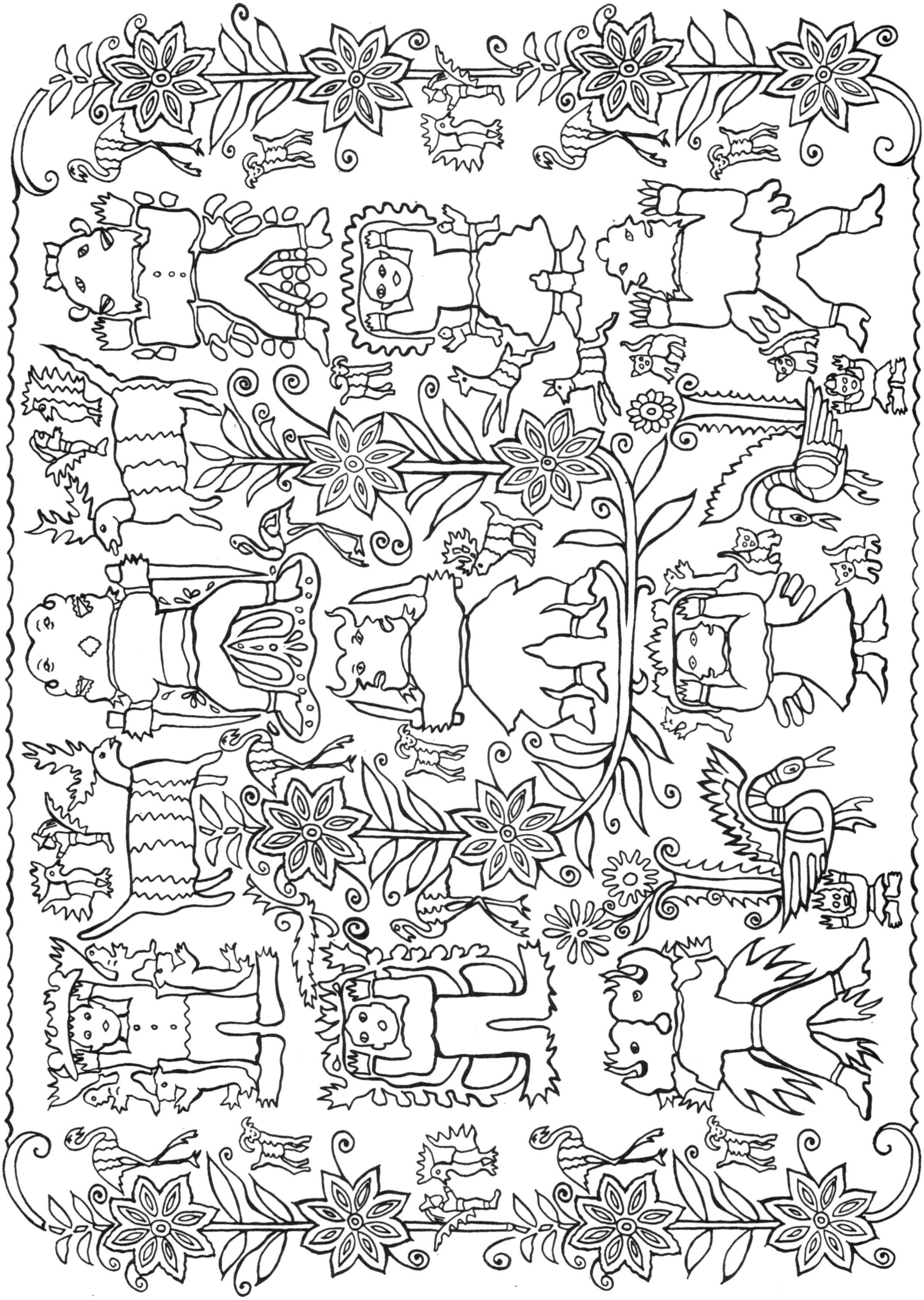

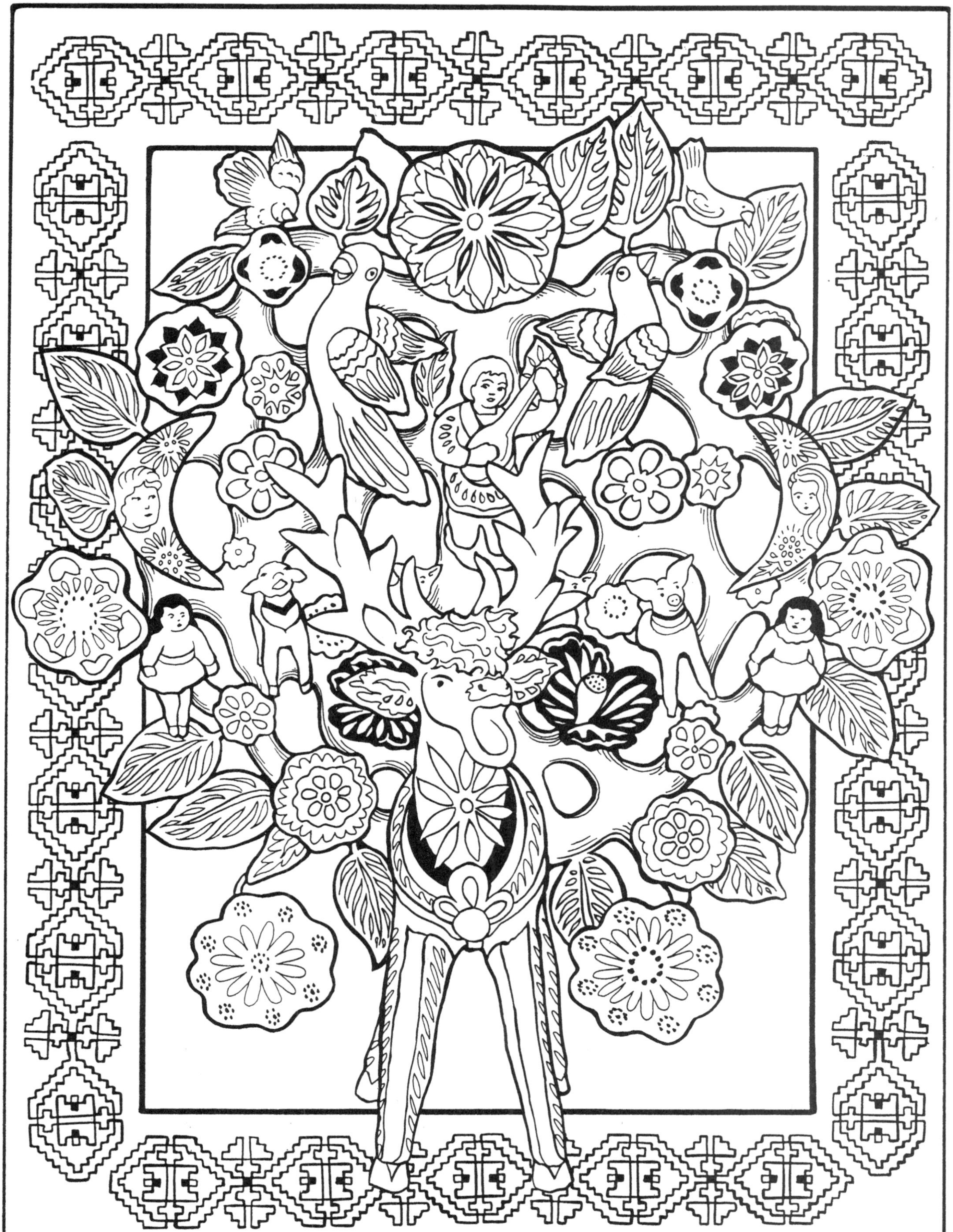

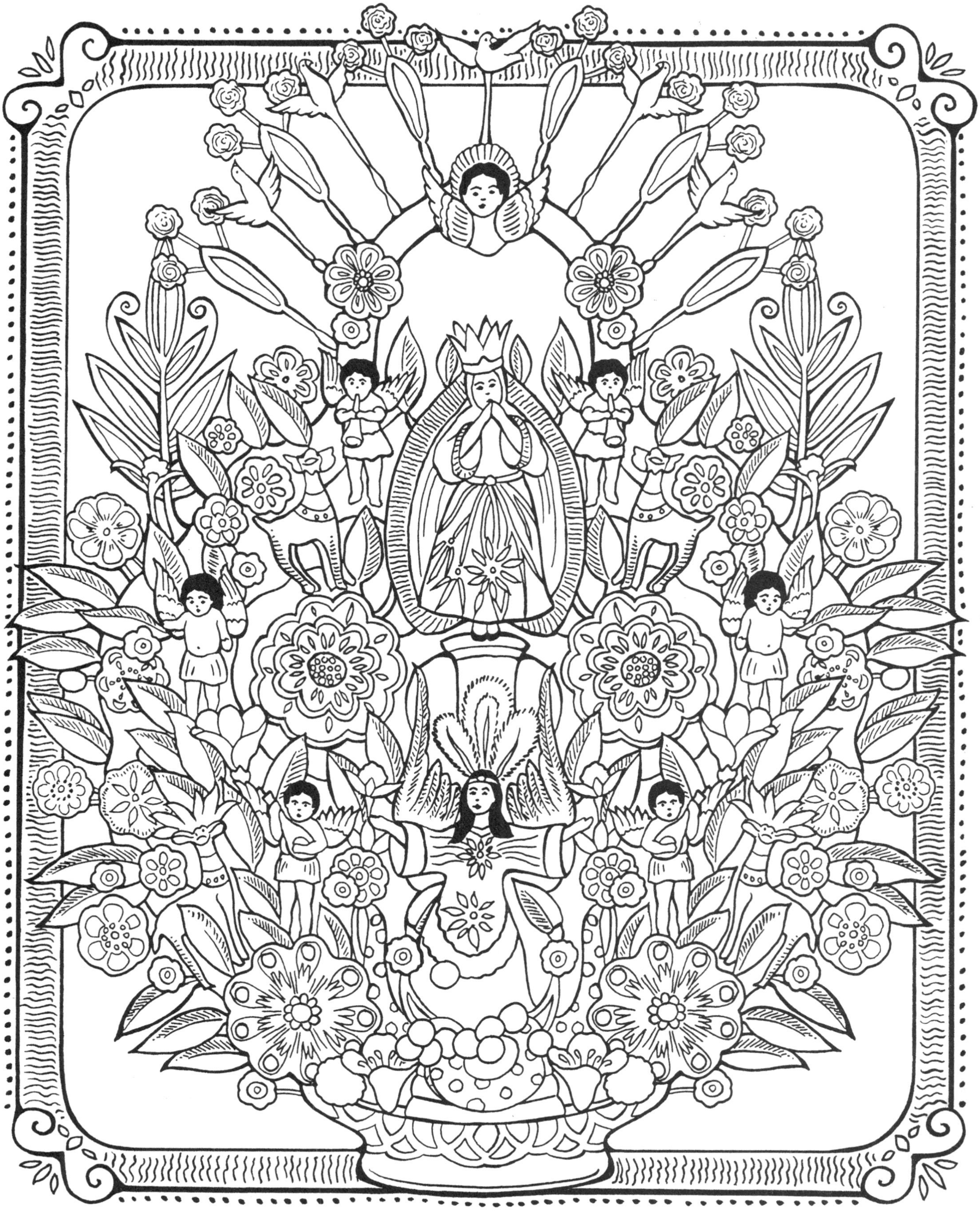

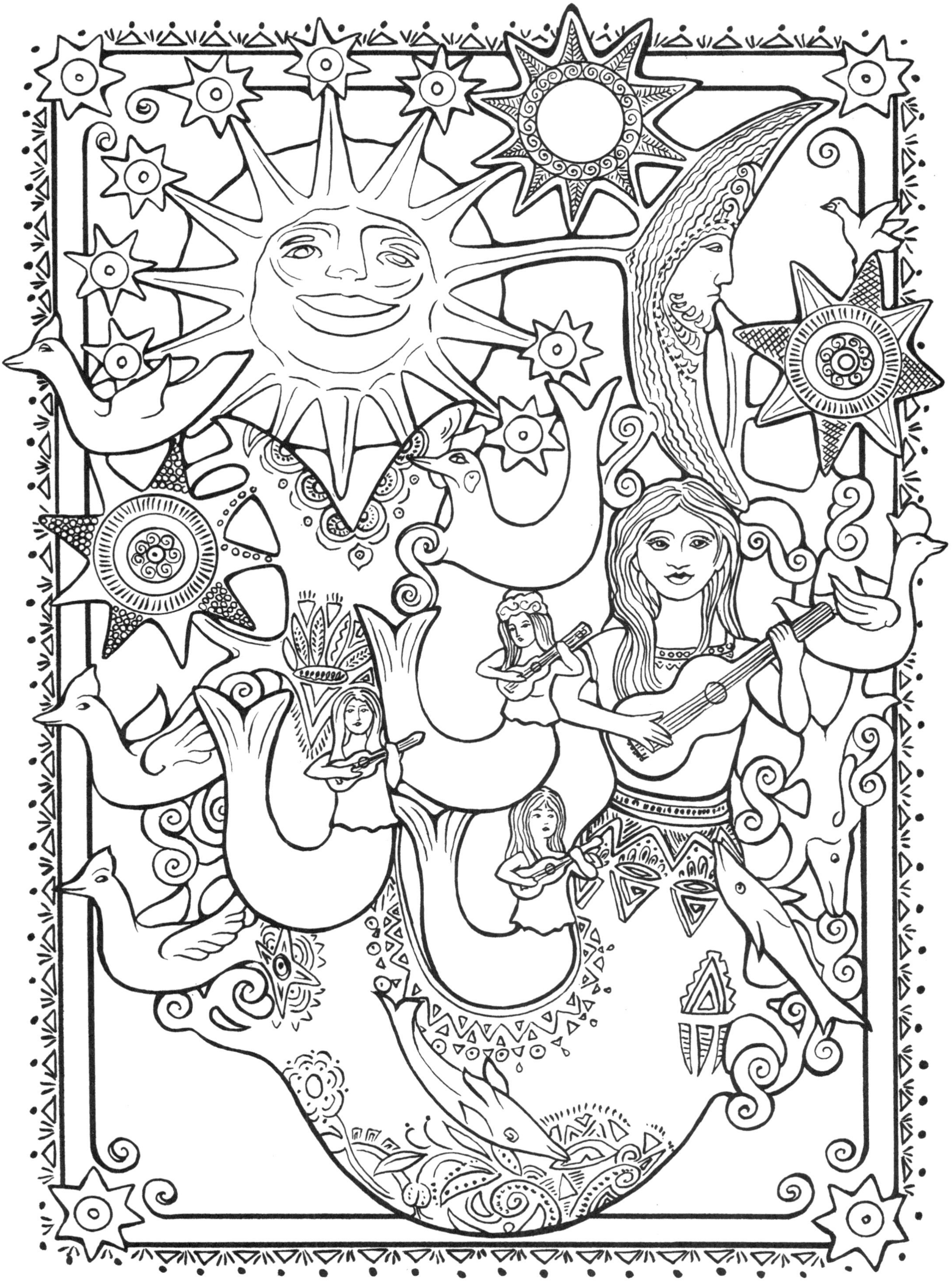

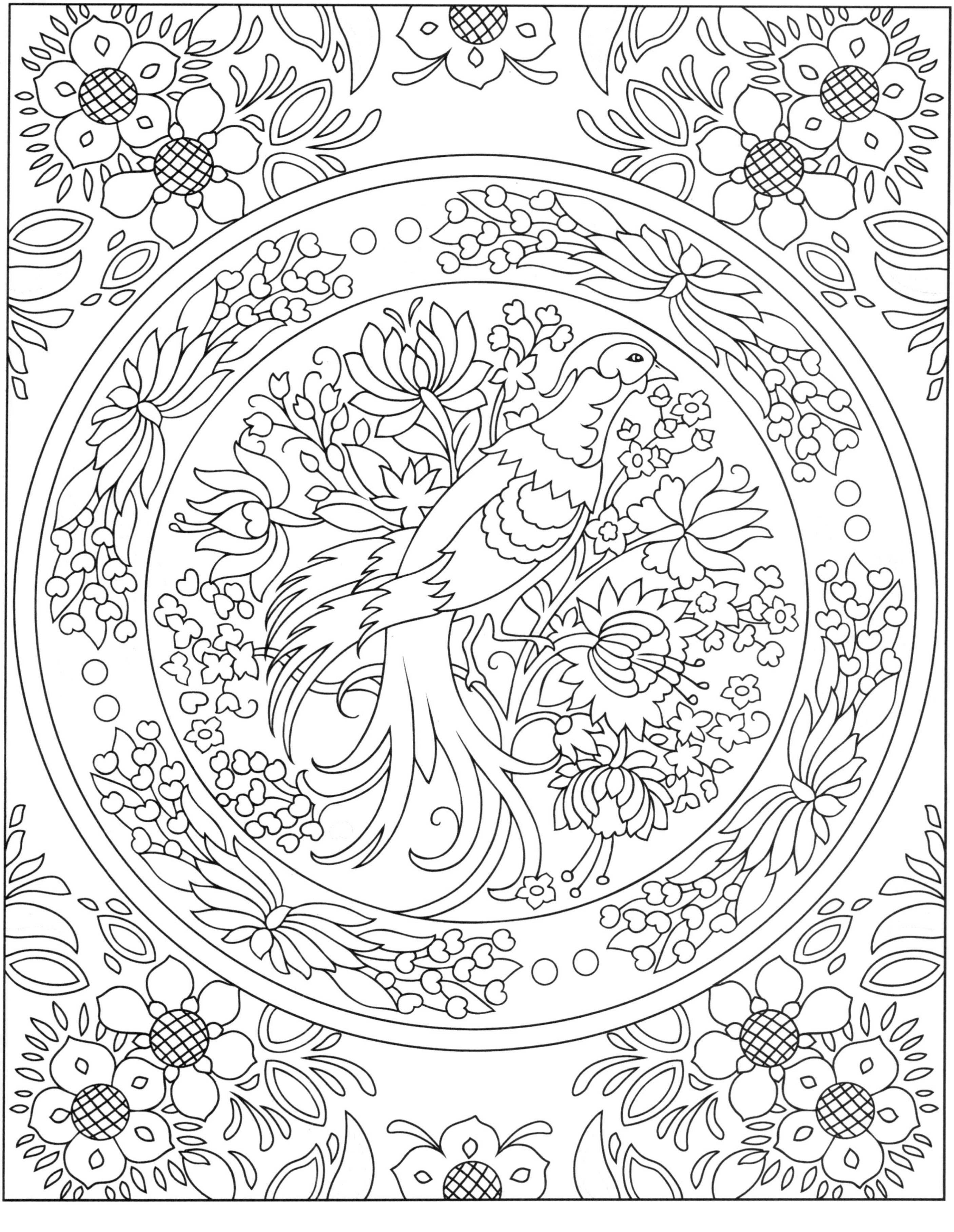